D0571967

LIVING BEYOND THE DAILY GRIND

BOOK II

A NOTE TO THE READER

CHARLES R. SWINDOLL

REFLECTIONS ON THE SONGS AND SAYINGS IN SCRIPTURE

LIVING BEYOND THE DAILY GRIND

BOOK II

Guideposts®

CARMEL • NEW YORK 10512

Printed in the United States of America

It is with deep feelings of gratitude that I dedicate this volume to the men who served on the faculty at Dallas Theological Seminary during my years of training from 1959 to 1963.

Their competent scholarship, insightful instruction, unfailing dedication to Christ as Lord, and relentless commitment to the Scriptures as the inerrant Word of God have marked me for life.

CONTENTS

INTRODUCTION ix

SECTION THREE: THE SONGS IN SCRIPTURE
(Week 27 through Week 39) 245

Living Beyond the Grind of . . .
Ritual Religion (Psalm 63) 247
Enemy Attack (Psalm 91) 258
Ingratitude (Psalm 100) 275
Aimlessness (Psalm 101) 285
Sorrow and Grief (Psalm 116) 298
Low Enthusiasm (Psalm 119:1–8, 97–100) 309
Family Life (Psalms 127 and 128) 320
Impatient Arrogance (Psalm 131) 335
Lingering Consequences (Psalm 137) 345
Insignificance (Psalm 139:1–12) 355
Insecurity (Psalm 139:13–24) 366
Depression (Psalm 142) 379
Praise-less Times (Psalm 149) 389

SECTION FOUR: THE SAYINGS IN SCRIPTURE
(Week 40 through Week 52) 401

Living Beyond the Grind of . . .
Submission to Sovereignty (Proverbs 9:10–11; 10:3,
29; 16:7; 19:21; 21:1) 403

Laziness (Proverbs 12:24, 27; 13:4; 15:19; 18:9;
   19:15; 22:13; 26:13–16) 410
Imbalance (Proverbs 24:10; 30:7–9) 417
Opposition (Proverbs 1:20–22, 29–32) 423
Addiction (Proverbs 20:1; 23:29–35) 429
Revenge (Proverbs 17:5; 24:17–20; 25:21–22) 435
Envy (Proverbs 3:31–32; 6:34–35; 14:30; 23:17–19;
   24:1–2, 19–20; 27:4) 442
Intolerance (Proverbs 19:11; 24:11–12; 28:21; 29:7;
   30:11–14) 448
Excuse-Making (Proverbs 30:24–28) 455
Financial Irresponsibility (Proverbs 3:9–10; 10:22;
   16:16; 22:7, 26–27; 23:4–5; 28:19–20, 22) 462
Motherhood (Proverbs 31:10–31) 472
Displeasing God (Proverbs 6:16–19) 481
Substituting Knowledge for Wisdom
   (Proverbs 1:1–23) 486

CONCLUSION 493

NOTES 495

INTRODUCTION

Here is more good news for those who are struggling to live beyond the grinding hassles of everyday living. In this second volume of *Living Beyond the Daily Grind*, we pick up our year-long journey through selected Psalms and Proverbs at week twenty-seven, applying the soothing oil of these songs and sayings of Scripture to such daily difficulties as ingratitude, sorrow, excuse-making, praise-less times, envy, financial problems, motherhood, and many others.

When I began this project many months ago, I had no idea how extensive it would become. Now that I realize its broad dimensions, I find myself grateful for fresh strength to see it through to completion.

My approach in this second volume will be the same as in the first—practical and relevant rather than analytical and scholarly. From my experience of more than two and a half decades in ministry, I have learned that the quickest way to put the truth of Scripture into people's lives is both through their heart and through their head. This is especially true of the Psalms and the Proverbs. God has preserved these songs and sayings not simply for the purpose of intellectual stimulation but for their practical application as well. If we are ever going to put biblical principles into action, we must deliberately resist the temptation to substitute analysis for appropriation.

This is not to say that we should drift and dream our way through Scripture, spiritualizing this phrase or that, hoping that a few ideas will inadvertently lodge in our minds like floating sticks snagged on a river bank. On the contrary, God's Book deserves our serious concentration as we seek to apply its wisdom to the nagging and inescapable pressures with which we live. At the same time, however, we must not miss the beauty of its poetry as we pursue the practicality of its message. Keeping this balance can be tricky.

In one of his lesser known works, *Reflections on the Psalms,* C. S. Lewis addresses the need for this balance that I am attempting to describe. I could not agree more with his observations.

> In this book, then, I write as one amateur to another, talking about difficulties I have met, or lights I have gained, when reading the Psalms, with the hope that this might at any rate interest, and sometimes even help, other inexpert readers. I am "comparing notes," not presuming to instruct. . . .
>
> What must be said, however, is that the Psalms are poems, and poems intended to be sung: not doctrinal treatises, nor even sermons. Those who talk of reading the Bible "as literature" sometimes mean, I think, reading it without attending to the main thing it is about; like reading Burke with no interest in politics, or reading the *Aeneid* with no interest in Rome. That seems to me to be nonsense. But there is a saner sense in which the Bible, since it is after all literature, cannot properly be read except as literature; and the different parts of it as the different sorts of literature they are. Most emphatically the Psalms must be read as poems . . . if they are to be understood; no less than French must be read as French or English as English. Otherwise we shall miss what is in them and think we see what is not.

The approach we took in Book I will continue in this book as well—one reading a week, with an emphasis on carrying out the suggestions that appear in the Reflection section at the end of each reading. The first thirteen weeks will focus on selections from the Psalms, and the last thirteen weeks, on the Proverbs.

I commend you for your faithful diligence. There are many who graze through the Bible in a random manner, nibbling here and yon with only a passing interest in words on a page. Few are those who drink deeply and consistently from the streams of living water. May our Lord richly reward you for your commitment. Ultimately, may He use the pages that follow to help you to continue living beyond the daily grind.

Chuck Swindoll
Fullerton, California

THE SONGS IN SCRIPTURE

WEEK 27
THROUGH
WEEK 39

$\mathcal{P}$SALM

A Psalm of David, when he was in the wilderness of Judah.

O God, thou art my God; I shall seek Thee earnestly;
My soul thirsts for Thee, my flesh yearns for Thee,
In a dry and weary land where there is no water.
Thus I have beheld Thee in the sanctuary,
To see Thy power and Thy glory.
Because Thy lovingkindness is better than life,
My lips will praise Thee.
So I will bless Thee as long as I live;
I will lift up my hands in Thy name.
My soul is satisfied as with marrow and fatness,
And my mouth offers praises with joyful lips.

When I remember Thee on my bed,
I meditate on Thee in the night watches,
For Thou hast been my help,
And in the shadow of Thy wings I sing for joy.
My soul clings to Thee;
Thy right hand upholds me.

But those who seek my life, to destroy it,
Will go into the depths of the earth.
They will be delivered over to the power of the sword;
They will be a prey for foxes.
But the king will rejoice in God;
Everyone who swears by Him will glory,
For the mouths of those who speak lies will be stopped.   [63:1–11]

THE GRIND OF
RITUAL
RELIGION

How easy it is to fall into the trap of "ritual religion"! So many Christians know little of a vital, fresh, day-by-day relationship with the Lord. I did not say an *inactive* relationship. Christians have never been more active! The tyranny of the urgent is no theoretical problem. Many a believer leaves the treadmill of three or more activities every Sunday only to enter a full week of meetings, appointments, functions, rehearsals, clubs, engagements, banquets, studies, committees, and retreats. I heartily agree with the one who said:

> Much of our religious activity today is nothing more than a cheap anesthetic to deaden the pain of an empty life![1]

I write not out of bitterness but out of a deep desire that we cultivate a consistent and meaningful walk with the Lord Jesus Christ—one that exists without needing to be pumped up and recharged with unending activities. I would wish that we all might know our Lord in such a significant way that this divine companionship, this healthy vertical relationship, knows fewer and fewer ups and downs. We *must* find ways to live beyond the grind of ritual religion that is devoid of a personal, daily relationship with the Lord.

In *The Pursuit of God*, perhaps his finest book (my second copy is almost worn out), A. W. Tozer points out:

I want to deliberately encourage this mighty longing after God. The lack of it has brought us to our present low estate. The stiff and wooden quality about our religious lives is a result of our lack of holy desire. Complacency is a deadly foe of all spiritual growth. Acute desire must be present or there will be no manifestation of Christ to His people. He waits to be wanted. Too bad that with many of us He waits so long, so very long, in vain.

Every age has its own characteristics. Right now we are in an age of religious complexity. The simplicity which is in Christ is rarely found among us. In its stead are programs, methods, organizations and a world of nervous activities which occupy time and attention but can never satisfy the longing of the heart. The shallowness of our inner experience, the hollowness of our worship, and that servile imitation of the world which marks our promotional methods all testify that we, in this day, know God only imperfectly, and the peace of God scarcely at all.[2]

David's ancient song, Psalm 63, has to do with what it means to hunger, to thirst and long for God—to be fully satisfied with Him alone. It is not a song of activity but of quietness . . . not a song designed to give the drum beat to busy feet but to thirsty souls—genuinely hungry saints!

By the way, are you one? Have you finally come to the end of rat-race religion? Have you decided to leave the hurry-worry *sin*drome and find complete satisfaction in the Savior, in the worship of Him alone? If you have, you are rare. In fact, you are almost extinct! But, if you have, this ancient song is for you. If you have not, it will sound mystical, perhaps even dull. David's quiet song, you see, is written for the few who are still hungry—for those who prefer depth to speed.

SUPERSCRIPTION

Very simply, the superscription reads: "A Psalm of David, when he was in the wilderness of Judah."

David composed this ancient hymn. But he was not in a temple or a worshipful tabernacle; he was in the wilderness

. . . alone, removed, obscure, separated from every comfort and friend. He was acutely acquainted with thirst, hunger, pain, loneliness, and exhaustion—but these were not his basic needs, as we shall see.

EXPOSITION

As in many of the psalms, the first verse sets the tone and gives the composition its theme.

> O God, Thou art my God; I shall seek Thee earnestly;
> My soul thirsts for Thee, my flesh yearns for Thee,
> In a dry and weary land where there is no water.

Right away we see that he was not seeking literal food, water, comfort, or rest—he was seeking a deep communion with his Lord. The "dry and weary land" is a vivid picture of our world today. So few, so very few believers are living victoriously. So many, so very many in this world are captivated with "stuff" and the pursuit of more and more. As a result, the inner barren-ness of soul is beyond belief. The land is indeed "dry and weary," but that only makes the yearning stronger! Since "there is no water" in that kind of land, David longs for his thirst to be quenched from above.

The next verse begins with "Thus." This is a very significant connective. The idea here is "So then . . ." or "Therefore. . . ." David longs for God. Nothing around him can satisfy that long-ing. He says, in effect, "So then, since nothing around me culti-vates a sense of closeness and companionship, I will cultivate it myself." Actually, the *Thus* of verse 2 introduces several things David does to satisfy his inner longing for a deep walk with his Lord. I find *five specific things* the songwriter does to find such satisfaction. They appear in the balance of his song:

1. He mentally pictures the Lord (v. 2).

> Thus I have beheld Thee in the sanctuary,
> To see Thy power and Thy glory.

When he says, "I have beheld Thee," we understand he means just that; he perceives his glorious Lord in his thoughts. The verse mentions the Lord's "power" and "glory." He imagines these things clearly in the thought processes of his mind. He spends time in the wilderness framing a mental picture of the Lord in power and glory on His heavenly throne. He takes the scriptures he knows regarding the Lord God and allows them to "sketch" in his mind a mental image of Him. In other words, he sets his mind upon and *occupies himself with the Lord.* That is a great way to remove the wearisome ritual from religion.

We all have vivid imaginations. In fact, these imaginations can get us into trouble if they are not kept under control. Ugly pride or lust, hatred or jealousy can feed our minds vivid pictures which can lead to terrible sins. This is precisely the case of "committing adultery in the heart" which our Savior mentions in Matthew 5:28. Lustful imaginings can ultimately result in illicit acts of passion.

David gives us a remedy: Spend those leisure moments picturing the Lord Himself. Or, in the words of the apostle Paul: "Set your mind on the things above, not on the things that are on earth" (Col. 3:2).

The next time you're tempted to allow your mind to paint the wrong mental picture, remember Psalm 63:2.

2. He expresses praise to the Lord (vv. 3–5).

> Because Thy lovingkindness is better than life,
> My lips will praise Thee.
> So I will bless Thee as long as I live;
> I will lift up my hands in Thy name.
> My soul is satisfied as with marrow and fatness.
> And my mouth offers praises with joyful lips.

I don't want to be spooky or come across the least bit vague about this matter of praise. Obviously, praise is important since the psalms are full of it. Look back over these verses. Verse 3 says it is something "my lips" do. In verse 5 they are "joyful lips." Verse 4 says it is to be done "as long as I live," so it isn't a once-a-week matter. An additional hint is given in verse 3, where God's "lovingkindness" prompts David to praise his Lord. Praise "satisfies his soul," according to verse 5.

Yes, praise is a deeply significant aspect of our personal worship, and we are remiss if we ignore it. Unfortunately, many are afraid of praise because they associate it with some sort of wild, uncontrolled, highly emotional "praise service," in which individuals faint, scream, jump around, and dance uncontrollably in the aisle. Listen, praise is important! It is not limited to public meetings or televised religious services. Praise is to flow from within us. Praise gushes forth and refreshes us. Actually, praise is an aspect of *prayer.* Let me explain:

Prayer could be divided into five parts:

a. *Confession* (read Prov. 28:13; 1 John 1:9). Dealing completely with sins in our lives—agreeing with God that such-and-such was wrong, then claiming forgiveness.
b. *Intercession* (read 1 Tim. 2:1–2). Remembering others and their needs in prayer.
c. *Petition* (read Phil. 4:6; Heb. 4:15–16). Bringing ourselves and our needs to God. Remembering them and requesting things of the Lord for ourselves.
d. *Thanksgiving* (read 1 Thess. 5:18). Prayer that expresses gratitude to God for His specific blessings and gifts to us.
e. *Praise* (read 1 Chron. 29:11–13). Expressions of adoration directed to God without the mention of ourselves or others—only God. We *praise* God by expressing words of honor to Him for His character, His name, His will, His Word, His glory, etc.

Husband, when you were dating your wife-to-be, can you remember doing this? You looked at her hair . . . and you expressed praise over her hair. You praised her for her beauty, her choice of perfume and clothing, and her excellent taste. You probably ate some of her cooking—and praised her for it. You observed the way she talked and expressed herself, and again you praised her. Praise came naturally because that was a genuine, stimulating part of romance. By the way, I hope you

haven't *stopped* praising her! Praise is greatly appreciated by
your wife, and likewise by our Lord. He frequently tells us in
His Word of its importance to Him.

   3. He meditates on the Lord (v. 6).

> When I remember Thee on my bed,
> I meditate on Thee in the night watches.

To meditate means "to muse, to ponder." According to Psalm
49:3, the mouth speaks wisdom but when the heart meditates
upon God's Word, *then* comes understanding.

I find it noteworthy that in this sixth verse David refers to
the night watches and being on his bed when he meditates.
This points up a very helpful fact. One of the best times to
ponder God's Word and allow the mind to dwell upon it is
when we retire at night. That's the time David said he remembered the Lord. Restless, fretful nights are calmed by moments
of meditation.

   4. He sings for joy (vv. 7–8).

> For Thou hast been my help,
> And in the shadow of Thy wings I sing for joy.
> My soul clings to Thee;
> Thy right hand upholds me.

David was in the wilderness. He had no audience, nor did
he seek one. God was the single object of his worship and it
was to Him his soul would cling. To strengthen the relationship between himself and his Lord, David *sang* for joy. Rare
but blessed are those disciples of David who are relaxed
enough in God's presence to break forth in song. Singing
brings joy to our hearts.

One of my most unforgettable experiences having to do
with a song sung in solitude occurred when I was in the
Marine Corps, stationed on Okinawa. A missionary, whom I
had come to appreciate because of his spiritual investment in
my life, was undergoing a severe, crucial trial. I knew of it
because he had shared it with me. I watched him to see how
he would respond. He didn't seem discouraged nor did he lose

his zeal. One evening I went to his home and was told by his wife that he was down at his little office in Naha, the capital city. I took the bus that rainy night and arrived a couple of blocks from his office. Stepping off the bus, I began splashing my way toward his office. Before long I began to hear singing. I realized it was his voice. The hymn was familiar. I remember the words so clearly:

> O to grace how great a debtor,
> Daily I'm constrained to be!
> Let Thy goodness, like a fetter,
> Bind my wandering heart to Thee. . . .[3]

It was my missionary friend, singing before his Lord all alone at his study-office. It was at times like that he found strength and joy in the midst of his trials. He had learned the truth of this verse in Psalm 63. In "the shadow of [God's] wings" my friend sang for joy. As I listened I felt as if I were standing on holy ground.

5. <u>He rejoices in his God (vv. 9–11).</u>

> But those who seek my life, to destroy it,
> Will go into the depths of the earth.
> They will be delivered over to the power of the sword;
> They will be a prey for foxes.
> But the king will rejoice in God;
> Everyone who swears by Him will glory,
> For the mouths of those who speak lies will be stopped.

David closes this psalm of worship with a pen portrait of his situation. To our surprise, he wasn't absolutely alone, because verse 9 testifies of those who sought his life to destroy it. Nor was he free from criticism and slander, according to the last verse. But the most surprising of all is that small portion that reads: "But the king will rejoice in God. . . ."

Who will soon be king? David! He is saying that the threatening circumstances would not steal his joyful spirit. As the king-elect, he would not doubt his Lord's protection. What an enviable determination!

Are you as determined as young David to live beyond the grind of religious ritual? I encourage you to cultivate such a spontaneous relationship with your God that you never again fall into the predictable mold of empty religion. Once you have tasted the real thing, you'll never be satisfied with plateaus of phony piety. You will want only to be in "God's presence," regardless of your location. It is the most refreshing place to be on Planet Earth, even though, at the time, you may find yourself "in the wilderness."

EFLECTIONS ON RITUAL RELIGION

1. Can you define "ritual religion"? How does it differ from true spirituality that includes authentic worship and meaningful praise? Describe the contrast in these two columns:

Ritual Religion	True Spirituality

2. Evaluate your religious activities for the next few minutes. Make a mental list of your weekly schedule. After naming each one, ask some hard questions:

   • Is this vital to my relationship with Christ?
   • Does this encourage me to grow deeper in my walk?
   • Am I doing this for the right motive?
   • What would happen if I stopped this activity?
   • Should I? Am I really willing to do so?

3. Deliberately change some longstanding habits for the purpose of adding freshness to your relationship with Christ.

   • Drive to church a different route.
   • Change your time of meeting with the Lord each day this week.
   • Pray after a meal instead of before it.
   • Sit in a different place at church on Sunday.
   • Add a hymn or praise song to your devotions.
   • Use another version of the Scripture for a month.

   See what a creature of habit you have become without realizing it?

PSALM

He who dwells in the shelter of
   the Most High
   Will abide in the shadow of the
   Almighty.
I will say to the Lord, "My refuge and my
   fortress,
My God, in whom I trust!"
For it is He who delivers you from the
   snare of the trapper,
And from the deadly pestilence.
He will cover you with His pinions,
And under His wings you may seek
   refuge;
His faithfulness is a shield and bulwark.

You will not be afraid of the terror by
   night,
Or of the arrow that flies by day;
Of the pestilence that stalks in darkness,
Or of the destruction that lays waste at
   noon.
A thousand may fall at your side,
And ten thousand at your right hand;
But it shall not approach you.
You will only look on with your eyes,
And see the recompense of the wicked.
For you have made the Lord, my refuge,

Even the Most High, your dwelling place.
No evil will befall you,
Nor will any plague come near your tent.

For He will give His angels charge
    concerning you,
To guard you in all your ways.
They will bear you up in their hands,
Lest you strike your foot against a stone.
You will tread upon the lion and cobra,
The young lion and the serpent you will
    trample down.

"Because he has loved Me, therefore I
    will deliver him;
I will set him securely on high, because
    he has known My name.
He will call upon Me, and I will answer
    him;
I will be with him in trouble;
I will rescue him, and honor him.
With a long life I will satisfy him,
And let him behold My
    salvation." [91:1–16]

THE GRIND OF
ENEMY ATTACK

Enemy attack? I can imagine a few of you who just read these words are saying to yourself, "sounds pretty treacherous to me. . . . But I'm not sure I know much about such things." I understand. There was a time in my life when I would have entertained similar thoughts. No longer, however. You may be surprised to know that there are many in God's family who have encountered demonic assaults, especially those who have served Christ in regions where the powers of darkness are commonplace. But in no way are enemy attacks limited to those dark corners of the world.

My wife and I have often talked about how we can sense the invisible presence of the adversary. There are subtle yet distinct hints that evil forces are at work. There is a heaviness in one's spirit, a lingering realization that what we are dealing with is more than another human being could be causing. Usually there are unexplainable coincidences and at the same time superhuman feelings of oppression that bear down on the mind. We have noticed that during such attacks our attempts to pray for relief are strangely thwarted. It's eerie! There aren't necessarily noises in the night or furniture moving across the floor, but sleep is often disturbed. A breaking free from the insidious attack is beyond one's own ability to make happen. Wicked, vile thoughts (even suicidal promptings) can accompany these assaults. There is no mistaking the source—the enemy of our souls is behind such ungodly grinds in life. How grateful I am for this song in Scripture. It, like few other scriptural passages, comes to grips with enemy attacks and gives us hope to get beyond them.

Every ancient song, like every great hymn, has its own special "tone." The magnificent hymn "And Can It Be?" has a tone of *assurance.* The lovely "Guide Me, O Thou Great Jehovah" has a tone of *dependence and trust.* The moving strains of "O Sacred Head, Now Wounded" carry a tone of *passion and pain,* while "I Am His, and He Is Mine" conveys *love and acceptance.* Psalm 91 has a unique tone in its message as well. We discover this by reading it through and looking for words or phrases that communicate similar thoughts. Let me list some:

Verse 1:   *shelter*
Verse 2:   *refuge . . . fortress*
Verse 4:   *refuge . . . shield*
Verse 5:   *terror by night . . . arrow . . . by day*
Verse 6:   *pestilence . . . destruction*
Verse 7:   *a thousand may fall*
Verse 9:   *refuge*
Verse 11: *guard*
Verse 15: *rescue*

There can be little doubt about the "tone" of Psalm 91; it is warfare, battle, conflict, fighting. It is a song for battle in that it conveys an atmosphere of daily, oppressive enemy attack.

Who is the enemy? Israel's national foes? No. A human being who is opposing the writer? I don't believe so. An actual, visible war on a bloody battlefield? No, I doubt it. Look at several more verses as we identify the enemy:

Verse 3:   *the trapper*
Verse 8:   *the wicked*
Verse 10: *evil*

Then consider the promise of angelic assistance (vv. 11–12) as well as divine deliverance (vv. 14–15).

I firmly believe that this song deals with our spiritual

enemies, *the Devil and his demons*. It talks about a battle in the unseen spiritual realm. This explains our need for angelic and divine intervention. Because our enemy, in this case, is supernatural in strength, we need supernatural help. This also helps us understand the promise of *absolute* deliverance from "the pestilence" that stalks day and night . . . and the *full* protection that is provided us (vv. 5–7). I find no other explanation, realistic or accurate, for these verses defy defeat. In no other realm could we claim such absolute protection and deliverance.

I hesitate to spell out the full spectrum of enemy attacks. Neither space nor time to explain all the details are sufficient. But perhaps an example or two would help. There are certain people whose presence throbs with evil. Being near them unleashes depressing powers which are both frightening and unavoidable. I have encountered these individuals throughout my ministry and have never forgotten the attacks. Frequently the people have trafficked in mind-bending occult practices and/or have been heavily involved in the drug culture. I have seen weird, even bizarre things occur in my family during such times. Fitful nightmares, passionate outbursts of rebellion and arguments, a heavy cloud of depression, strange accidents, and uncharacteristic marital disharmony can follow in the wake of these attacks. I shudder as I recall those awful times.

Keep this in mind as we dig into Psalm 91. The tone is *warfare* and the enemy is our evil adversary who comes at us with persistent regularity.

OUTLINE

Let me suggest four distinct parts to Psalm 91:

I. Protection amid Evil (vv. 1–4)
II. Attitude toward Evil (vv. 5–10)
III. Assistance against Evil (vv. 11–13)
IV. Security from Evil (vv. 14–16)

PROTECTION AMID EVIL

Because the first four verses are crucial to the rest of the psalm, let's take our time as we develop them.

A very important fact to remember is that we as believers in the Lord Jesus Christ are not removed from the *presence* of wickedness. In fact, our Savior prayed specifically: "I do not ask Thee to take them out of the world, but to keep them from the evil one" (John 17:15).

This verse alerts us to a significant truth—God has planned that we continue to live in a hostile, wicked, non-Christian world system (*kosmos*) but be protected all the while. He deliberately did not remove us from an atmosphere of hostility.

As I mentioned earlier, He has made possible a plan of *insulation* not *isolation*. God isn't interested in our isolating ourselves, hidden away like pious hermits in a cave, but rather that we live courageously on the front lines, claiming His insulation amid an evil environment.

Now then, in order for us to enjoy the benefits of insulation, we must live in the light of Psalm 91:1–4. The secret, of course, is in our *dwelling* in the shelter of the Most High—our abiding in His shadow habitually.

The word *dwells* (v. 1) is translated from the Hebrew *yah-shaav*, meaning "to remain, sit, abide." There is a permanence conveyed in the original term. We would say, "live in conscious fellowship with, draw daily strength from—let Him habitually have first place." That is the applied truth of the Hebrew text. The idea is developed further with the mention of "the shelter" in verse 1. This original word is *sah-thaar*, meaning "cove, covert, secret hideaway." It is therefore a place of vertical nearness and divine intimacy.

Before going any further, let me emphasize that Psalm 91 is written to *dwellers*. It promises deliverance and protection not to everyone, but to *dwellers*, those who draw daily, habitual strength from their Lord as they sustain an intimacy of fellowship and nearness with Him. Don't forget that!

We are told in the last part of verse 1 that as this close

fellowship is maintained, we shall ". . . abide in the shadow of the Almighty." Now we come upon a different Hebrew term translated *abide*. It is *loon*, meaning "to lodge, pass the night." It conveys a periodic rest or stopover for lodging.

What is verse 1 actually saying? Simply this: If we who know the Lord Jesus Christ will dwell in conscious fellowship with Him (keeping our sins confessed and forsaken, and walking in moment-by-moment dependence upon Him), we shall enjoy the benefits of living under His protective care on those occasions when rest and lodging are needed. If we maintain our walk with Him, we can count on Him and His deliverance at periodic times when the going gets rough.

This explains why verse 2 says:

> I will say to the Lord, "My refuge and my fortress,
> My God, in whom I trust!"

A "refuge" is a place of rest. A "fortress" is a place of defense. Notice that this does not say the Lord will *provide* these things. Rather, it says that the Lord *is* these things. This is why our dwelling in Him is essential . . . because it is *in Him* alone that we will find rest and defense. Take time to consider the last word in verse 2—*trust*. It is a translation of the same Hebrew term as the one in Proverbs 3:5 which we studied in the previous volume.

> Trust in the Lord with all your heart,
> And do not lean on your own understanding.

It means a total trust, as if resting all one's weight on something else. When one is crippled, he must trust his crutches. That is the kind of trust our Lord wants from us.

Verses 1 and 2 deal with who God is, but verses 3 and 4 deal with what God does. Basically, there are three things named:

a. He delivers: from the snare of the trapper and
                 from the deadly pestilence
b. He covers: with His pinions/under His wings
c. He shields: by His faithfulness

The Hebrew sentence structure enables us to point out particular emphases in our study from time to time. In this case, the emphatic part of verses 3–4 is "He." The New American Standard Version renders it, ". . . it is He. . . ." The idea is emphatic: "He, alone" or "He it is, not anyone else!" Practically speaking, you will find no absolute assistance or deliverance from anyone else—only your Lord in whom you trust.

Now, one at a time, let's look at the specific things He provides for us in times of enemy attack.

1. He delivers from the snare of the trapper.

I want to remind you once again that this promise is directed to the "dweller." Not everyone—not even every Christian—is promised deliverance. If you wish to be delivered, you must dwell! If you are now under satanic/demonic assault, the way to deliverance is dwelling—drawing power and triumph through His name and His victory at Calvary. I shall deal with the specifics of this later.

Look at the word *deliver*. It is translated from *nah-tzaal*, meaning "to snatch away." This original term appears in Psalm 34:19: "Many are the afflictions of the righteous; / But the Lord *delivers* him out of them all" (emphasis mine).

How great is His deliverance!

This third verse goes on to say that we will be "snatched away" from a "snare." Literally, it means a "bird trap." My Webster's dictionary says that a trap is ". . . something by which one gets entangled, something deceptively attractive. . . ."

But remember, we need not be victims! It is He alone—our glorious, all-conquering Lord—who "snatches us out" as we dwell in Him.

He delivers also from "the deadly pestilence." Literally, "from a death of destruction." One translation renders this "from a violent death." This, of course, is the ultimate result of our being ensnared. Never doubt it; the devil plays for keeps. If possible, he will take us to a violent death, as Saul, who took his own life (1 Sam. 31:4; 1 Chron. 10:13–14) and Judas, who did the same (Luke 22:3; Matt. 27:5). Satan's ultimate desire is our destruction. He is happy when a self-inflicted, violent death smears the testimony of a Christian. Our Lord promises deliverance from such a death.

2. He covers with His pinions/under His wings.

The Lord is here pictured as an immense bird keeping close watch over its brood. Both Psalm 36:7 and Psalm 57:1 mention the protection we have under our Lord's "wings." The prophet Isaiah includes God's promise that we are dearer to Him than a nursing child is to his mother (49:15–16). What comfort!

Back in the nineteenth century, William O. Cushing put this vivid word picture into a poem:

> Under His wings I am safely abiding;
> Though the night deepens and tempests are wild,
> Still I can trust Him:
> I know He will keep me;
> He has redeemed me, and I am His child.
>
> Under His wings, under His wings,
> Who from His love can sever? . . .[4]

3. He shields by His faithfulness.

The psalmist has pictured our Lord's protection in three distinct ways in verses 3 and 4. First, in the scene of a trapper. Second, in the scene of a bird and her brood. Now, in the scene of a battle. Here he assures us that we are guarded by His faithful presence.

Now let's consider the balance of this psalm.

ATTITUDE TOWARD EVIL

I find two invincible attitudes we are to exhibit toward evil:
1. No fear (vv. 5–6).

> You will not be afraid of the terror by night,
> Or of the arrow that flies by day;
> Of the pestilence that stalks in darkness,
> Or of the destruction that lays waste at noon.

Look over the descriptive terms that portray our enemy's tactics: *terror . . . arrow . . . pestilence . . . destruction.* All these describe satanic and demonic assaults against us. Notice also that these assaults take place at any time of the day or night. Our enemy will stop at nothing to make us afraid! Intimidation is one of his sharpest darts.

Child of God, we need not fear! Martin Luther was right when he wrote:

> And tho' this world, with devils filled,
> Should threaten to undo us;
> We will not fear, for God hath willed
> His truth to triumph through us:
> The prince of darkness grim,
> We tremble not for him;
> His rage we can endure,
> For lo! his doom is sure,
> One little word shall fell him![5]

The late, great Charles Haddon Spurgeon's comment is equally reassuring:

> When Satan's quiver shall be empty thou shalt remain uninjured by his craft and cruelty, yea, his broken darts shall be to thee as trophies of the truth and power of the Lord thy God![6]

2. Faith (vv. 7–10).

> A thousand may fall at your side,
> And ten thousand at your right hand;
> But it shall not approach you.
> You will only look on with your eyes,
> And see the recompense of the wicked.
> For you have made the Lord, my refuge,
> Even the Most High, your dwelling place.
> No evil will befall you.
> Nor will any plague come near your tent.

I see *faith* written between each line, don't you? Our Lord expects us to stand firmly on His Word—His promises—His strength. Read Ephesians 6:10–11, 16 at this juncture, my friend. You'll see that the "shield of faith" is able "to extinguish *all* the flaming missiles of the evil one" (emphasis mine). Remember, faith demands an *object*. Like love and mercy, faith cannot exist alone. In this case, faith's object is God's written Word. Our Lord and Savior has recorded His truth for us to claim when the going gets rough. Nothing else can hold us together and keep us from panic in the way that specific verses and passages of written Scripture do. If you fail to set your heart upon God's Word, you'll soon weaken in your resistance and ultimately succumb to the traps of the enemy. You will have to fight ignorance and superstition and even a few of your uneasy feelings if you're going to walk by faith, child of God.

There are at least four specific biblical truths for the Christian to claim when undergoing or seeking release from satanic/demonic attacks.

1. The Cross. Go to verses that declare Satan's defeat at Calvary. Read them orally: Colossians 2:13–15, Hebrews 2:14–15, and 1 John 3:8.

2. The Blood. As you consider and claim Satan's defeat at the Cross, call to mind specific passages dealing with the *blood* of the Lord Jesus Christ: Romans 5:8–9 and Revelation 12:10–11.

3. The Name. As you seek deliverance and strength amid your battle, verbally state the *full name* of the *Lord Jesus Christ* as your refuge and sovereign God: Proverbs 18:10 and Philippians 2:9–10.

4. The Word. Stand firmly upon God's written Word, as our Lord did when the Devil tempted Him to yield to his traps: Matthew 4:4, 7, 10 and Ephesians 6:11, 17.

If you will use this as a practical guide and claim each one *by faith,* you will be among the righteous ones who are *bold as a lion* (Prov. 28:1), and you will find that you can live beyond the grind of enemy attacks.

ASSISTANCE AGAINST EVIL

For He will give His angels charge concerning you,
To guard you in all your ways.
They will bear you up in their hands,

Lest you strike your foot against a stone.
You will tread upon the lion and cobra,
The young lion and the serpent you will trample down (Ps.
   91:11–13).

These verses assure us of angelic assistance when we face attacks from supernatural realms. It makes sense. Satan and the demons are supernatural beings—so are angels. We need supernatural help when dealing with supernatural enemies. By the way, for further information on angels, read Psalm 103:19–21 along with Hebrews 1:14.

Now let's look closely at verses 11–13. The psalmist states three distinct activities of the angels on our behalf.

1. Angels are given "charge" of us (v. 11). The term *charge* is from the Hebrew *tzah-wah*, which means "to appoint, install, give command of." Angels are actually *appointed* to us, given command of certain earthly individuals. Consider Matthew 18:10. It reads:

See that you do not despise one of these little ones, for I say to you, that their angels in heaven continually behold the face of My Father who is in heaven.

Give some thought to the possessive "their." In other words, children have *their own* angels—unseen guardians—who are actually *appointed* by God. The same is true of adults (Acts 12:15). We have been appointed angelic assistance. In numerous yet invisible ways, they come to our aid.

2. Angels "guard" us in all our ways (v. 11). The Hebrew *shah-maar* means "to keep, watch over, observe, preserve, take care of." Angels are overseers of God's people. Like silent sentries, they stand guard over us, preserving our steps.

My wife and I frequently smile as we call to mind those days when our four active children were young. How very, very busy the angels must have been who were assigned to them! I am personally convinced they heaved a sigh of relief when our children finally grew from the age of endless, reckless activity to a more mature lifestyle. Believe me, we frequently thank the Lord that we had at least four unseen baby sitters who assisted us twenty-four hours a day, seven days a week back then!

3. Angels "bear you up" in their hands (v. 12). The verb *nah-sah* actually means "to lift, to carry, take up." Here in Psalm 91 it means "to support, sustain." This rounds out the picture, doesn't it? Angels are appointed to us, and they watch over us, preserving us and guarding us from demonic assault. At times, it is necessary for them to support and sustain us, even as Elisha and his servant were assisted in 2 Kings 6:15–17 (please stop and read).

SECURITY FROM EVIL

We have almost finished this rather extensive journey through Psalm 91. For thirteen verses the songwriter has been speaking. Now, *God* speaks . . . the Lord declares six "I wills":

> I will deliver him (v. 14).
> I will set him securely on high (v. 14).
> I will answer him (v. 15).
> I will be with him in trouble (v. 15).
> I will rescue him and honor him (v. 15).
> I will satisfy him (v. 16).

What a list of promises! Child of God, these are addressed to *you*. Look at that initial phrase and concluding phrase in verse 14: "Because he has loved Me . . . because he has known My name." The Lord says that those who love Him and those who know Him have this secure hope in Him. The Hebrew term used for "love" is unusual and rare. Most often it is used with reference to "attaching something to something." The Hebrew term includes the idea of attaching a saddle to a horse. It would be acceptable to render Psalm 91:14: "Because he clings affectionately to Me. . . ."

The Lord's "I wills" are not for everybody. But then, they weren't meant to be. God gives these promises to dwellers, "clingers," believers who, by faith, wrap themselves around their Savior. What a way to live! As a matter of fact, it's the *only way to live!*

CONCLUSION

May I ask: Do *you* know the Lord Jesus Christ personally? Has there ever been a time in your life when you took Christ at His Word and asked Him to take over the controls of your life, to enthrone Himself within you? He wants to be your Lord and Savior, but He waits for your decision. He really doesn't want you to perish. He wants to satisfy you with a meaningful, full, abundant life. Won't you invite Him in right now? Act now. The Lord Jesus Christ is ready to enter your life. Just utter a prayer of invitation as soon as you conclude this study. Don't delay. Please receive Christ now. When you have Him living within, no enemy attack will ever again have the power to overcome you.

EFLECTIONS ON ENEMY ATTACK

1. Even though our examination of this great song was lengthy and a bit detailed, I don't want you to miss its practical relevance. Like few other scriptures, it addresses the believer's assurance of victory over our adversary's attacks. You may be going through the grind of demonic oppression. There may be a person whose presence is clearly an evil force in your life. You may be fighting off thoughts of injuring yourself or taking your own life. Perhaps you got involved in the world of occult practices years ago and you still fight those forces from the past. What an exhausting battle that can be! Remind yourself of two wonderful facts:

   • You have no reason to fear.
   • Your faith will overcome all enemy attacks.

   Repeat those two statements again and again.

2. You may need even more reassurance. Turn back to this magnificent song and circle the three promises God gives you.

   Verse 10a: No evil will befall you.
   Verse 10b: No plague will invade your home.
   Verse 11: Angelic assistance will guard you.

Remind yourself of those three promises as you retire for a night's rest this very evening. The enemy of our souls prefers "night attacks," so don't be surprised if he uses the darkness to frighten you.

3. Read this psalm aloud and in its *entirety* each day this week. Along with the psalm, read Romans 8:31–39 and 1 John 4:4; 5:18–21. Literally, *claim those truths* today. This is a heavy subject, but one we need to deal with without any uneasiness.

*P*SALM

A Psalm for Thanksgiving.

Shout joyfully to the Lord, all the
earth.
Serve the Lord with gladness;
Come before Him with joyful
singing.
Know that the Lord Himself is God;
It is He who has made us, and not we
ourselves;
We are His people and the sheep of His
pasture.

Enter His gates with thanksgiving,
And His courts with praise.
Give thanks to Him; bless His name.
For the Lord is good;
His lovingkindness is everlasting,
And His faithfulness to all
generations.   [100:1–5]

THE GRIND OF INGRATITUDE

In these days of abundance and wealth, it is our tendency to become ungrateful and presumptuous. Affluence abounds in our American culture. Many a family has a driveway full of cars, a house full of gadgets, appliances, personal television sets and telephones, and a refrigerator full of food. Life isn't simply easy-going, it's downright luxurious!

Please don't misunderstand. Having an abundance is not a sin, in and of itself. Throughout the pages of Scripture we find examples of people who were both wealthy and godly: Abraham, Job, Joseph, David, Solomon, Josiah, Barnabas, Lydia, to name a few. But we also find some who became enamored of their wealth and lost sight of the Lord and His right to rule their lives. As I have said on numerous occasions, there is nothing wrong with having nice things . . . but there is everything wrong when nice things have us. Ingratitude and presumption can quickly rob our lives of generosity and humility. Here is a song that will bring back a spirit of thankfulness and joyful gratitude.

Every time I read through the One Hundredth Psalm, I think of Vacation Bible School! Do you have the same reaction? For some reason I was memorizing all or part of Psalm 100 every summer of my childhood in VBS. As I think of that, I also remember the three Bible school teachers who resigned when they learned they would have *me* in their department! Needless to say, I was not a "model child" in church. Take heart, Sunday school teachers! You could be teaching a potential pastor as you labor with a group of busy, noisy children. I thank God for those who were longsuffering with me!

Psalm 100, however, is not just a "Bible school psalm." Nor is it directed to children only. As we take a closer look at this favorite old hymn, three questions come to mind.

Question One: *To whom is it addressed?* Read verses 1 and 5 once again. You'll find that it is addressed to *all the earth* (v. 1), to *all generations* (v. 5). Psalm 100 is for the whole world—all ages and stages. It is broad in its scope. Its message is universal. We are to understand that God wants *all* people in every era to hear and apply its message.

Question Two: *Of whom does it speak?* Verses 1–3, along with verse 5, give us the answer. Psalm 100 speaks of *the Lord.* His name appears no less than four times. One of those times He is declared to be God Himself. This psalm directs our attention to *Jehovah,* the Old Testament personal name for God. You cannot appreciate Psalm 100 (nor can you apply its message) if you are not intimately acquainted with the One of whom it speaks. Being thankful—really thankful—begins with being rightly related to the Giver of everything.

Question Three: *How is it arranged?* Let your eyes graze back over the lovely meadow of this psalm. Do you notice its arrangement? Since the Psalms were originally written as hymns, they are poetic in form. That doesn't mean they rhyme, but it does mean that they follow a certain style, a "meter" or "beat." Each psalm is independent of all the others. Like our present-day hymns, each one has a distinct message and arrangement.

Psalm 100 is composed of seven commands or imperatives. Following these commands a final verse appears that sums up God's character, giving us the reason for the commands. Let's work our way through the psalm by keeping this arrangement in our minds.

THE COMMANDS

1. Shout joyfully to the Lord.

This is quite a beginning! In fact, the Hebrew is very explicit, leaving out the term "joyfully," for literally it says: *Shout to the*

Lord! The word *shout* comes from a Hebrew word meaning "to raise a shout, to give a blast" (as on a trumpet). In our modern day we use certain terms to express approval:

Right on!	Fantastic!
Far out!	Wonderful!
All right!	Praise God!
Great!	Amen!

These are "shouts" or verbal expressions of thanksgiving. God says to all the earth-dwellers, "Shout words of joyful approval to me!"

Haven't you come to realize this? At certain times God does things about which we cannot keep quiet. He takes care of little details or some problem, and we suddenly sense that He has come to our assistance. Don't accept this silently. Shout to Him. Lift up your voice in praise! By doing so we counteract that grind of ingratitude that so easily can climb aboard.

2. Serve the Lord with gladness.

A healthy sign of the grateful life is *serving*. Few things do a better job of interrupting the daily grind of ingratitude than serving others. Ponder this portion of God's Word. In doing God's work, we serve Him, not the local church, not the superintendent of some department, not the pastor or some board. We serve the Lord. It is *He* we worship and for *Him* we labor— not man! And please observe that this kind of service is not irksome, nor does it come from guilt. The verse says it is *with gladness*. The Hebrew term for this phrase was used when talking about pleasant things that gave happiness.

How very, very rare it is to find service with gladness in churches today. Many people serve in order to relieve their guilt or to quiet their conscience. Some serve because they feel obligated or forced. The vast majority of Christians think only in terms of service in a local church and miss the concept of serving Christ's Body—the universal church. Yet the Body has needs, aching needs, numerous needs, many of them outside particular local church functions.

There is the service of encouragement, fellowship, giving (time as well as cash), being involved with others in helping those who are in need, discipleship, sharing the Lord, bearing others' burdens, and on and on. Oh, that gladness might characterize our service!

3. <u>Come before Him with joyful singing.</u>
We have already considered this idea of singing on several occasions, so there is no need to add much to my previous remarks. Let me simply emphasize the word *joyful*. I get the picture that God prefers to have us happy people, rejoicing in His presence, for He has mentioned it in each line of this psalm thus far.

Are you joyful? Really now, is your face pleasant—is a smile frequently there? Do your eyes reveal a joyful spirit within? When you sing, in church for example, is it *with joy?* The next chance you get, glance at the fellow in the next car on the freeway. He is *never* smiling! Look at the lady ahead of you or behind you at the grocery store. No smile . . . no joy.

I was humming and smiling the other day as I was shopping and several people stared at me! One even asked why I was happy. I had a choice opportunity to talk about why I was happy and to share with him the One who gave me joy.

Lighten up, Christian! Dress up your testimony with a genuine spirit of joy! Happiness is truly contagious.

4. <u>Know that the Lord Himself is God. . . .</u>

> Know that the Lord Himself is God;
> It is He who has made us, and not we ourselves;
> We are His people and the sheep of His pasture. [v. 3]

Our worship of the Lord God is to be intelligent. We are to *know* certain things in order for this to be true. This third verse lists three things we need to keep in mind:

• *We are to know that God is our Lord.* We quickly acknowledge Christ as our Savior—but so slowly do we submit ourselves to Him as our *Lord.* Immediately, He accepts us into His family as we believe He died and arose for us . . . but only after years of stubborn struggling it seems, do we finally allow Him *first place* as our sovereign Lord. We are to know that the One we worship is the Lord, our God.

• *We are to know that He has made us.* I see two things of practical importance here. First, God made, designed, and formed us just as we are. We are to keep that in mind. We look precisely like He planned for us to look. He made us, inside and out, literally. No person can joyfully live his life and shout praises to God until he accepts himself as God has made him. Second, God is still "making" us—He is not through. We are not self-made people. No one is! A wonderful thought is tucked away in the first part of Philippians 2:13. I want to quote from *Kenneth Wuest's Expanded Translation:* "For God is the One who is constantly putting forth His energy in you. . . ."[7]

You see, God is still working. He is not finished by any means, child of God. Please cooperate. Please be patient.

• *We are to know that we are His sheep, that we belong to Him.*

It is awfully easy to want to be the shepherd. So, we must be reminded that we are His sheep; we belong to Him. He is in charge. As sheep, we are to submit.

5. Enter His gates with thanksgiving, and His courts with praise.

What was in the psalmist's mind? To what do the "gates" and "courts" refer? I believe he had the *temple* in mind. That was the place where he approached God's presence, for God's glory literally filled the temple, according to 2 Chronicles 5:14 and 1 Kings 8:10–11. The temple had its gates and its courts, both of which gave access to the presence of God.

Today we have no such earthly phenomena. In light of that, how do we enter His gates and His courts? What is our access to His presence today? The answer is *prayer*. Hebrews 4:16 invites us to "draw near" to God's throne. Through prayer we come into the very presence of God. And this psalm tells us to do it with two things accompanying our coming—thanksgiving and praise.

6. Give thanks to Him.

Because this sixth command is so closely linked with the fifth, I mention it before applying the point. Giving thanks is repeated so that we will not miss its importance.

If you're looking for "signs of the last days," you will probably not think of looking for *ingratitude,* but you should. It is listed in 2 Timothy 3:1–5 right along with the more popular and obvious "signs." We have become an ungrateful, thankless generation! Small wonder God repeats the importance of giving thanks in Psalm 100.

7. Bless His name.

The word *bless* is from *bah-rack,* meaning "to kneel." The idea is to show honor and homage to God—His name is higher than any other name on earth.

REASONS FOR THE COMMANDS

For the Lord is good;
His lovingkindness is everlasting,
And His faithfulness to all generations. [v. 5]

Why obey these seven commands? The answer is connected to His character:

Because He is good.

Verse 3 told us "He is God" and this final verse tells us "He is good." The original Hebrew term, *tobe* means "pleasant, agreeable, delightful." How different from the present-day concept many people have of God. He is not an irritated Sovereign of heaven who takes delight in smashing our lives and frowning on our happiness—like some celestial Bully with a club in His hand. No! He is good. His commands are best for us. His ways are perfect.

Because His lovingkindness is everlasting.

God loves and accepts us as we are. Knowing what will best encourage us and give us real happiness, He leads us into His way by giving us His commands in this song. His unqualified love and acceptance are behind His every command.

Because He is faithful forever.

He is not partial. The God who commands is fair and faithful to *all* generations. He doesn't play favorites. His commands will result in benefits (if obeyed) because He is faithful.

Turn, finally, to Ephesians 5:1. Read the verse slowly. *The Amplified Bible* renders it: "Therefore be imitators of God—copy Him and follow His example—as well-beloved children [imitate their father]."

It is not enough to read that God is pleasant, agreeable, loving, accepting, faithful, and impartial. *We are to mimic our Father!* In fact, we are *commanded* to do so in Ephesians 5:1. Why not start today? Give up your self-centered way of life and stretch your spiritual wings! God, by His indwelling Holy Spirit, longs to live out His character through you . . . and He longs to start right now. As He does so, the grind of ingratitude will slowly fade into oblivion.

EFLECTIONS ON INGRATITUDE

1. In your own words, define gratitude.

   _____

   _____

   _____

2. Do a little reviewing of the things God has provided for you. In the words of the old gospel song, "Count your many blessings, name them one by one." List some of them below. You'll be surprised how it will help you live beyond the grind of ingratitude.

   Blessings at home:

   Blessings at church:

   Personal blessings:

Take the time throughout the week to express your gratitude to God. Your cup is full and running over, isn't it?

3. Don't limit your gratitude to God. Think about five or six people who have meant much to you. Before the week has run its course, write each one a note of appreciation. Express your thanks briefly but sincerely. For all you know, one (or more) of them could be going through an intensely difficult trial at this very moment.

A Psalm of David

I will sing of lovingkindness and
    justice,
To Thee, O Lord, I will sing praises.
I will give heed to the blameless way.
When wilt Thou come to me?
I will walk within my house in the
    integrity of my heart.
I will set no worthless thing before my
    eyes;
I hate the work of those who fall away;
It shall not fasten its grip on me.
A perverse heart shall depart from me;
I will know no evil.
Whoever secretly slanders his neighbor,
    him I will destroy;
No one who has a haughty look and an
    arrogant heart will I endure.

My eyes shall be upon the faithful of the
    land, that they may dwell with me;
He who walks in a blameless way is the
    one who will minister to me.
He who practices deceit shall not dwell
    within my house;
He who speaks falsehood shall not
    maintain his position before me.
Every morning I will destroy all the
    wicked of the land,
So as to cut off from the city of the Lord
    all those who do iniquity.   [101:1–8]

THE GRIND OF AIMLESSNESS

Some people seem to drift aimlessly through life, headed in no specific direction. Without clearly defined objectives, it is not surprising that many adopt a lifestyle that lacks definition and purpose.

I know a few folks who sort of take life as it comes . . . no big deal. Reminds me of the time I had been invited to a college campus to speak. On my way to the meeting hall, I met a fellow who was obviously apathetic. Hoping to put a little spark into his plans beyond graduation, I asked him a few probing questions. I'll never forget his answer to my first one: "Where are you going . . . what are your plans?" With hardly a hesitation, he answered back, "Plans? Well, uh, I'm going to lunch." How typical of those caught in the grind of aimlessness! They live from one meal to the next. Without much concern beyond that evening's television programs, they drift through life like a skiff in a swamp.

The psalmist chose not to live a life without purpose. Aside from David's slump into disobedience, he served the Lord as His man for many, many years. He was indeed "a man after God's own heart." For the most part, he lived a godly life. This brings us to Psalm 101. Perhaps more than any other passage of Scripture, these eight verses explain David's *spiritual philosophy of life*. In fact, an appropriate title for Psalm 101 might be: *David's Statement of Faith*. This song represents his credo. It declares his spiritual aims.

He committed himself to these things without reservation. Not that he never fell short, but he always had the standard before him. In this psalm there is not the slightest trace of diplomatic compromise or vacillation . . . only simple, straightforward, devout words. He subscribed to this "profession of faith," and in doing so he became God's man of the hour. All who hope to live beyond the grind of aimlessness would do well to observe how David declared himself. As before, we want to survey the psalm before working our way through it.

Psalm 101 could be called "the psalm of wills and shalls." I count at least ten "I wills" or "I shalls." This tells us that the psalm is very *personal*. In fact, it begins with a series of *resolutions* and ends with several *declarations.* Let's use Joshua 24:15 as the basis for our outline. It is the famous statement: ". . . choose for yourselves today whom you will serve: . . . but as for me and my house, we will serve the Lord."

For four verses David implies "as for me . . ." and lists his *resolutions* in five "I wills." Following that, in verses 5–8, he turns to his kingdom, implying "as for my house . . . ," and lists seven different types of people as he makes *declarations* about each one. An outline could look like this:

I. As for Me: Resolutions (vv. 1–4)
   A. I will sing (v. 1)
   B. I will give heed (v. 2a)
   C. I will walk (v. 2b)
   D. I will set (v. 3)
   E. I will know (v. 4)
II. As for My House: Declarations (vv. 5–8)
   A. Slanderer (v. 5a)
   B. Proud (v. 5b)
   C. Faithful (v. 6a)
   D. Blameless (v. 6b)
   E. Deceiver (v. 7a)
   F. Liar (v. 7b)
   G. Wicked (v. 8)

AS FOR ME: RESOLUTIONS

I once heard the president of a seminary express his concern over the school by saying, "I fear we may be turning out graduates with a great number of *beliefs* but not enough *conviction*." Conviction gives beliefs a backbone. David wasn't satisfied with a nice set of theological beliefs floating around in his head; he pinned them down to concrete convictions. It's as though he is saying in verses 1–4, "I'm committed to this purpose. . . ." In these four verses he lists four great qualities the believer *must* possess in order to maintain clear direction. Each one *assaults* an aimless mindset.

Consistency

> I will sing of lovingkindness, and justice,
> To Thee, O Lord, I will sing praises. [v. 1]

Observe what he sings about: lovingkindness and justice. For both of these things he expressed praise. I suggest that "lovingkindness" has reference to times of blessings, prosperity . . . the "good life." It would include times when all is going well. The "justice," on the other hand, suggests times of adversity, difficulty, and problems . . . the "real life." For both of these experiences, David praised his God. He resolved that he would be *consistent* in his praise no matter what his circumstances might be.

How important it is to be consistent in our praise to God! We are quick to sing praises to Him when we enjoy good health, financial success, happiness, freedom from pressure, and accomplishing some enviable achievement . . . but rarely do we praise Him for "justice," for the hard times when our tunnel of troubles seems so long.

On the heels of losing virtually everything, Job remained consistent. He remarked: "Shall we indeed accept good from God and not accept adversity?" (Job 2:10).

He refused to be fickle and inconsistent. To Job the Lord was to be praised as much for "taking away" as for "giving" (Job

1:21). Like Job, David resolved to be consistent in his praise to
God, whether times were good or bad.

Integrity

> I will give heed to the blameless way.
> When wilt Thou come to me?
> I will walk within my house in the integrity of my heart
> [Ps. 101:2]

The first part of this verse has to do with *public* integrity as
David says, literally, "I will give heed unto the way of integrity."
You may recall that the original Hebrew term translated *integrity* means "to be finished, whole, complete." It carries with it
the idea of being totally honest, thoroughly sound. The king of
Israel knew that his life before the people *had* to be solid and
honest for the kingdom to remain strong.

The second part of this verse has to do with *private* integrity—he mentions being sound in "my house" and "my
heart." Integrity is like an iceberg in that what shows is only a
very small part of the hidden whole.

Humility

> I will set no worthless thing before my eyes;
> I hate the work of those who fall away;
> It shall not fasten its grip on me. [v. 3]

David resolves to remove everything that might catch the affection of his heart and turn his gaze off the Lord and onto
himself. He claims that he will not allow a single thing to capture his attention and tempt him to exalt himself. He resolves
to avoid every unworthy aim and ambition. To do less would
inevitably lead to his "falling away" from fellowship with his
Lord.

Pride is such a senseless sin! It defies logic for any Christian
to be arrogant and gripped in the jaws of conceit. Paul implies
this in 1 Corinthians 4:6–7, which says:

Now these things, brethren, I have figuratively applied to myself and Apollos for your sakes, that in us you might learn not to exceed what is written, in order that no one of you might become arrogant in behalf of one against the other.

For who regards you as superior? And what do you have that you did not receive? But if you did receive it, why do you boast as if you had not received it?

Read that again! Whatever you and I have we were *given.* Since we were given that particular thing, why boast as though we deserve the credit? Of the seven things God says He hates (Prov. 6:16–19), can you remember the *first* on His "hit list"? It is "haughty eyes" . . . that arrogant, proud appearance which God says He will abase (Ps. 18:27).

Years ago I learned a little poem (source unknown). It puts us in our place, especially when we begin to think of ourselves as indispensable:

Sometime when you're feeling important,
Sometime when your ego's way up,
Sometime when you take it for granted that you are the
    prize-winning 'pup';
Sometime when you feel that your absence would leave an
    unfillable hole,
Just follow these simple instructions,
And see how it humbles your soul.
Take a bucket and fill it with water,
Put your hand in it up to your wrist.
Now pull it out fast and the hole that remains is the measure of
    how you'll be missed.
You may splash all you please as you enter,
And stir up the water galore,
But STOP and you'll find in a minute,
It's back where it was before.

Purity

A perverse heart shall depart from me;
I will know no evil. [v. 4]

David has resolved thus far that he will be a man of consistency, integrity, and humility. Now he resolves to be a man of purity—knowing no evil. This has to be one of the reasons God called David "a man after My own heart." Rare indeed are those people in this world who could say what David says in this fourth verse.

David's son Solomon also wrote of the value of personal purity in Proverbs 11:19–21:

> He who is steadfast in righteousness will attain to life,
> And he who pursues evil will bring about his own death.
> The perverse in heart are an abomination to the Lord,
> But the blameless in their walk are His delight.
> Assuredly, the evil man will not go unpunished,
> But the descendants of the righteous will be delivered.

Don't miss the last part of that passage. A pure life is actually a spiritual investment, the dividends being enjoyed by your children. God has a *purity layaway plan* . . . which you establish now and your descendants later cash in on.

I cannot overemphasize the value of a pure life. We have an inordinate curiosity about perversion and evil. We are not only aware of wickedness, but we are drawn to it with interest. The news media capitalize on this interest by highlighting the evil in our world. They have found that public interest is high when it comes to impure, wicked activities. David realized, however, that "a perverse heart" would only lead to a weakening of his spiritual life.

My wife, Cynthia, and I know a young man who was in training for the ministry. He met and married a girl who had been gloriously saved out of an impure past. She had been a call girl, a harlot of the street, connected with an organized ring of prostitutes in a large city. During those years she went to the depths of wickedness and shame. Through a series of events, she heard the gospel and came, by faith, to Christ. After her conversion and subsequent marriage to our minister friend, she found herself in an entirely new environment. Instead of evil there was purity and wholesome living. On one occasion, she shared with

Cynthia the tremendous adjustment she faced and the difficulty of fully forgetting her past. She wanted to, but evil had a way of lingering in her mind. Perhaps that is the reason David resolved to "know no evil." This world's system puts a brand upon us that is the next thing to impossible to erase. How much better it is to be pure and inexperienced than to be scarred by impure memories that are quick to play back their reruns at a moment's notice.

AS FOR ME AND MY HOUSE: DECLARATIONS

Now the composer changes direction. David no longer looks *within*, he looks *around*. He considers the people of his kingdom and declares his position regarding several different types . . . seven in all.

Slanderer

Whoever secretly slanders his neighbor, him I will destroy. [v. 5a]

The term *destroy* comes from a Hebrew word meaning "to put an end to." The idea is that David would put an end to and silence the slanderer. He would not tolerate slander!

Proud

No one who has a haughty look and an arrogant heart will I endure. [v. 5b]

David also declares that he cannot abide an arrogant person. You will notice that pride reveals itself in the *face*, "a haughty look . . . " but its source is in the *heart*, "an arrogant heart." Proverbs 21:4 (please read) also links the proud heart with a haughty appearance.

One of the practical problems connected with pride is dealing with its byproduct: *argumentation.* Show me a proud person—

really haughty—and I'll show you one who brings contention and arguments into almost every situation. Pride must have its say and its way! Listen again to Solomon, the wise: "Through presumption comes nothing but strife" (Prov. 13:10).

Faithful

> My eyes shall be upon the faithful of the land. [Ps. 101:6a]

While David couldn't endure the proud, he longed to dwell with the faithful of the land. He had discovered that the faithful person is usually easy to get along with . . . cooperative . . . teachable . . . and best of all, trustworthy.

I came across an interesting thought in my study of the Scriptures. On two occasions in the Book of Proverbs the same question is asked—once with regard to men and the other with regard to women.

The question: Who can find? The thought behind the question: This is so rare, you can hardly find one! Now look at Proverbs 20:6 for the *man*, then Proverbs 31:10 for the *woman*. Among men it is hard to find *faithfulness* ("who can find a trustworthy man?"). Among women it is hard to find *strength of character* (the literal meaning of the original word translated "excellent" in Proverbs 31:10—"an excellent wife who can find?").

Blameless

> He who walks in a blameless way is the one who will minister to me. [Ps. 101:6b]

David admits that there is a certain category of people who minister to him, who serve him. He says that they are the "blameless" people—not perfect but people of integrity.

In my opinion, this is the single most important trait to be found among ministers—among all those who minister, counsel, teach, and serve others. Integrity is absolutely indispensable in the lives of God's servants. When integrity breaks down, one forfeits the right to lead in a high-profile capacity.

Deceiver

> He who practices deceit shall not dwell within my house. [v. 7a]

David's original term for *dwell* in this verse is different from the previous verse. Here it means "to come near." He is saying that the hypocrite/deceiver will not even *come near* his house. Deception has to do with keeping back the full story or hiding the real motive behind an action. It is the act of deliberately causing someone to be misled. If you have ever dealt with a deceiver, you know why David felt so strongly about this.

Liar

> He who speaks falsehood shall not maintain his position before me. [v. 7b]

The king had a policy: No liar will be established in a position of authority! He would not tolerate lying.

By the way, this is a good business policy. You are unwise if you tolerate an employee in your business who is a liar. Perhaps you have tried to work with a liar. If so, you know the impossibility of sustaining a harmonious, secure relationship in that situation.

Wicked

> Every morning I will destroy all the wicked of the land,
> So as to cut off from the city of the Lord all those who do
>   iniquity. [v. 8]

This is quite a conclusion! He has mentioned several types of people and forcefully declared himself regarding each one, but this is the strongest of all. It seems certain that David believed in capital punishment. He knew that it was a God-ordained principle established once and for all as a definite tool to be used by government to maintain law and order (Gen. 9:5–6).

We live in a day when society is often blamed for the crimes of lawbreakers—felonies and misdemeanors alike. And even parents have been seen as guilty for their children's crime. Our whole basis of judgment has shifted from the objective, clear-cut assertions of Scripture to the subjective, shifting sands of human viewpoint and feeling. Oh, that we might return as a nation to God's truth, God's methods, God's pattern of dealing with those who do iniquity!

Well, there you have it—David's credo. There was no question as to where he stood on things that matter. With simplicity and objectivity, he stated his convictions. Aimlessness was not a word in his vocabulary, nor should it be in ours.

 EFLECTIONS
ON AIMLESSNESS

1. Is aimlessness one of the "daily grinds" you can't seem to shake? See if you can figure out why. Uncertain about your career? Disturbed over a few unwise decisions? Preoccupied with the fear of taking a risk? Talk this over with someone you respect. Do that this week for sure. Ask the individual to pray for you . . . to trust God with you that He would clarify your objectives and give you a sense of renewed assurance.

2. Select a person in history you admire because of his or her accomplishments. Go to the library and check out a copy of that person's biography. Read it during the next several weeks, taking special note of how the individual became focused in his energy and direction. Make a few notes of your own. We are often stimulated by the example of those we admire. Strong leaders are usually readers of biographies.

3. What a powerful "statement of faith" is Psalm 101! David wrote his in the form of a song. Let me challenge you to write out your own credo. First, think through where you stand . . . those areas that have no "wobble room" in your list of convictions. Then, write them down.

Here is my statement of faith:

I resolve:

I declare:

I love the Lord, because He hears
  My voice and my supplications.
  Because He has inclined His ear to
    me,
Therefore I shall call upon Him as long
  as I live.
The cords of death encompassed me,
And the terrors of Sheol came upon me;
I found distress and sorrow.
Then I called upon the name of the Lord:
"O Lord, I beseech Thee, save my life!"

Gracious is the Lord, and righteous;
Yes, our God is compassionate.
The Lord preserves the simple;
I was brought low, and He saved me.
Return to your rest, O my soul,
For the Lord has dealt bountifully with
  you.
For Thou hast rescued my soul from
  death,
My eyes from tears,
My feet from stumbling.
I shall walk before the Lord
In the land of the living.
I believed when I said,
"I am greatly afflicted."

I said in my alarm,
"All men are liars."

What shall I render to the Lord
For all His benefits toward me?
I shall lift up the cup of salvation,
And call upon the name of the Lord.
I shall pay my vows to the Lord,
Oh may it be in the presence of all His
    people.
Precious in the sight of the Lord
Is the death of His godly ones.
O Lord, surely I am Thy servant,
I am Thy servant, the son of Thy
    handmaid,
Thou hast loosed my bonds.
To Thee I shall offer a sacrifice of
    thanksgiving,
And call upon the name of the Lord.
I shall pay my vows to the Lord,
O may it be in the presence of all His
    people,
In the courts of the Lord's house,
In the midst of you, O Jerusalem.
Praise the Lord.   [116:1–19]

THE GRIND OF SORROW AND GRIEF

It is easy for those who are strong and healthy to forget how many tears of sorrow and grief are shed every day. All around this aching world—perhaps in your own home or in your heart this very week—sadness abounds. Tears fall. Grief has you in its grip. And it can happen so fast.

Just last week I spoke with a young man on our support staff at the church I serve as senior pastor. He was all smiles about his future, such a contagious fellow. But before nightfall that same day he was killed in an automobile-motorcycle collision. Today his family grieves his absence. Such is the groan of humanity. To omit the subject of sorrow and grief in a two-volume book on life's daily grinds would be inexcusable.

We don't know the details, but the composer of the ancient song you just read found himself in a grievous circumstance. Did you catch the clues as you read through his lyrics? He states that "the cords of death encompassed" him as well as "the terrors of Sheol" (the grave). He admits that he "found distress and sorrow" in whatever he was enduring. A few lines later he declares that he was "brought low" and the Lord rescued his "eyes from tears." Somehow his God put him back on his feet so firmly and brought back his perspective so clearly, he was able to write: "Precious in the sight of the Lord / Is the death of His godly ones" (Ps. 116:15).

Amazing! From the pit to the pinnacle . . . from agony to

ecstasy. The same one who begins the song in the dark valley of sorrow and grief (vv. 1–2) ends it in the most magnificent statement of praise a Jew could utter: "Hallelujah!" (v. 19, MLB).

The psalmist, after passing through the deep valley of grief, sits down and recounts his experience. The song is his personal testimony; first, of his love for the Lord who saw him through the turbulent waters of distress, sorrow, and grief (vv. 1–11); and second, of his desire to return his thanks to the Lord for seeing him through it all (vv. 12–19).

In outline form, the song could appear:

I. I love the Lord! (vv. 1–11)
   A. Because He hears me (vv. 1–2)
   B. Because He rescues me (vv. 3–6, 8–11)
   C. Because He cares for me (v. 7)
II. What shall I render to the Lord? (vv. 12–19)
   A. I shall proclaim His benefits (vv. 12–13)
   B. I shall pay my vows (vv. 14, 18–19)
   C. I shall praise His name (vv. 15–17)

I LOVE THE LORD!

Let's take a few moments this week to probe a little deeper into a song of sadness. To begin with, go back to that opening line, "I love the Lord, because . . ." (v. 1). In the nineteenth century a young English girl, Elizabeth Barrett, suffered a spinal injury at age fifteen, which left her a semi-invalid for many years afterward. Although she regained strength prior to her marriage to Robert Browning in 1846, she was hesitant to burden him with a frail, crippled wife. Her love for him was beautifully expressed in her work *Sonnets from the Portuguese* as she wrote the immortal words: "How do I love thee? Let me count the ways. . . ." She then held nothing back as she described the depth of her love. In the same way the psalmist says that to his Lord in his expressions of affection.

Why did he love the Lord? He counts the ways.

Because He Hears Me

> I love the Lord, because He hears
> My voice and my supplications.
> Because He has inclined His ear to me,
> Therefore I shall call upon Him as long as I live. [vv. 1–2]

1. He hears my voice.
2. He inclines His ear to me.

These are two distinct responses, not one and the same. The first, "He hears," simply means that when the psalmist speaks, God listens; God pays attention to what he has to say. The second, *He inclines,* is from the Hebrew *nahtah,* meaning "to bend, turn aside." It is more of an intimate term than *hear.*

For example, Solomon uses it in Proverbs 7:21 to describe the response of a man who is seduced by a harlot and "turns aside" to her. It appears in 1 Kings 11:4 to describe how Solomon's wives "turned away" his heart after other gods. The psalmist says that he loves the Lord because God "bends down," as it were, and "turns aside" from His infinite work . . . as He pays close attention to him in his sorrow and grief. God *never* turns His back on those who cry out to Him through tears. On the contrary, He "bends an ear."

Because He Delivers/Rescues Me

> The cords of death encompassed me,
> And the terrors of Sheol came upon me;
> I found distress and sorrow.
> Then I called upon the name of the Lord:
> "O Lord, I beseech Thee, save my life!"
> Gracious is the Lord, and righteous;
> Yes, our God is compassionate.
> The Lord preserves the simple;
> I was brought low, and He saved me. [vv. 3–6]

For Thou hast rescued my soul from death,
My eyes from tears,
My feet from stumbling. I shall walk before the Lord
In the land of the living. I believed when I said,
"I am greatly afflicted."
I said in my alarm,
"All men are liars." [vv. 8–11]

Some tragic circumstance had surrounded the writer. Some terrible, painful experience caused him to say that he was near death. Grief, sorrow, and difficulty were his companions, which explains why he confesses to a great deal of distress and even crying.

I believe Spurgeon best captures the pathos of the psalmist's situation as he writes:

> As hunters surround a stag with dogs and men, so that no way of escape is left, so was David enclosed in a ring of deadly griefs. The bands of sorrow, weakness, and terror with which death is accustomed to bind men ere he drags them away to their long captivity were all around him. . . . Horrors such as those which torment the lost seized me, grasped me, found me out, searched me through and through, and held me a prisoner. . . . these were so closely upon him that they fixed their teeth in him as hounds seize their prey.[8]

The marvelous part of it, however, is that the Lord delivered him; He rescued him. Though reduced in strength, slandered in character, depressed in spirit, sick in body, and grief-stricken, the psalmist testifies that the Lord stuck by his side! He always will. God doesn't ditch us; He doesn't leave the sinking ship; He doesn't retreat when the enemy increases strength. Our Lord is a specialist when it comes to deliverance, and you can claim that fact this moment!

We are not surprised to see that the psalmist says he will therefore "walk before the Lord" (v. 9) because of His deliverance. It is a natural reaction or desire to spend time with someone who stayed with us during some painful experience we endured.

Because He Cares for Me

> Return to your rest, O my soul,
> For the Lord has dealt bountifully with you. [v. 7]

Look at that! The words *dealt bountifully* are a translation of the Hebrew *gah-maal*, which means "to deal fully/completely" with something or someone. Frequently, it suggests the idea of "rewarding." Today we would say, "Because the Lord takes such good care of me, I will love Him in return." In other words, God leaves nothing out when He provides for us, when He takes care of us, when He surrounds us with His watchful care.

Having been lifted up and sustained in his grief, the songwriter then asks: "What shall I render to the Lord?"

WHAT SHALL I RENDER TO THE LORD?

In other words: How can I return my thanks? What will possibly suffice as proof of my gratitude? God has done so very, very much, how can I adequately render my appreciation to Him? How can I possibly repay? In response to that question, he offers three answers: (1) proclaim His benefits, (2) pay my vows, and (3) praise His name. Let's consider each one.

I Shall Proclaim His Benefits

> I shall lift up the cup of salvation,
> And call upon the name of the Lord. [v. 13]

What does "I shall lift up the cup of salvation . . ." mean? In the Old Testament the word *cup* is frequently used to denote plenty and abundance. You may remember that in Psalm 23:5 David claims that his "cup overflows." The term *salvation* actually appears in the Hebrew Bible in the plural—*salvations*. We would grasp the meaning better if we'd render it "deliverances." The psalmist is expressing praise to God for His abundant and numerous deliverances. So, literally, he says, "In the name of

Jehovah I shall proclaim." It is the idea of openly declaring that God is his Deliverer.

Moses does this in Deuteronomy 32:1–4:

> "Give ear, oh heavens, and let me speak;
> And let the earth hear the words of my mouth.
> Let my teaching drop as the rain,
> My speech distill as the dew,
> As the droplets on the fresh grass
> And as the showers on the herb.
> For I proclaim the name of the Lord;
> Ascribe greatness to our God!
> The Rock! His work is perfect,
> For all His ways are just;
> A God of faithfulness and without injustice,
> Righteous and upright is He."

This matter of making a public proclamation in honor of the Lord is important. It is good. It is healthy. It is biblical. God floods our lives with abundance . . . yet so few Christians share their experiences publicly, so few Christians "proclaim His benefits." (Unfortunately, we live in a day of spiritual secret-service agents. I sometimes think of them as Lady Clairol Christians: nobody knows but God!) Let's stop holding our praise to ourselves. Share your Savior . . . don't be ashamed or shy. If you want to render something of value to the Lord, proclaim His benefits! It may surprise you how much it helps you to live beyond the grind of sorrow and grief.

I Shall Pay My Vows

> I shall pay my vows to the Lord,
> O may it be in the presence of all His people, . . . [v. 14]

> I shall pay my vows to the Lord,
> O may it be in the presence of all His people,
> In the courts of the Lord's house,
> In the midst of you, O Jerusalem.
> Praise the Lord! [vv. 18–19]

A vow is a solemn promise to which you commit yourself before God. The vows found in the Bible are quite serious and binding. I also notice that biblical vows were always voluntary . . . but once made, they became compulsory. We may want to forget our vows today, but God never does.

The psalmist is saying that he can render his gratitude to the Lord by keeping his promises, preferably before the public. I recently discovered an excellent passage of Scripture regarding vows.

> Do not be hasty in word or impulsive in thought to bring up a matter in the presence of God. For God is in heaven and you are on the earth; therefore let your words be few. . . . When you make a vow to God, do not be late in paying it, for He takes no delight in fools. Pay what you vow! It is better that you should not vow than that you should vow and not pay. Do not let your speech cause you to sin and do not say in the presence of the messenger of God that it was a mistake. Why should God be angry on account of your voice and destroy the work of your hands? [Eccles. 5:2, 4–6]

Serious, isn't it? The Bible says that it is better not to vow at all than to vow and not keep your word.

I Shall Praise His Name

> Precious in the sight of the Lord
> Is the death of His godly ones.
> O Lord, surely I am Thy servant,
> I am Thy servant, the son of Thy handmaid,
> Thou hast loosed my bonds.
> To Thee I shall offer a sacrifice of thanksgiving,
> And call upon the name of the Lord. [Ps. 116:15–17]

Finally, the psalmist declares his thanks and praises God's name in appreciation for all His goodnesses. I have a question: Why does he mention "the death of His godly ones" here? I think the answer is connected to his tragic experience mentioned earlier in verses 3–4, 6, and 8. In fact, I believe the psalmist had been delivered from death, perhaps as a lone survivor. In verse 16, he mentions himself as "the son of Thy handmaid" from whom he had been "loosed." In other words, he had been loosed from the bonds of death, if I interpret this correctly. I suggest that the calamity and grief mentioned earlier quite probably snuffed out the life of several of his loved ones, quite likely including his mother—which resulted in his tears and grief (v. 8), sorrow and disillusionment (vv. 10–11). Even in these circumstances, he rendered his praise to God.

That is the way it ought to be. Our praise and thanksgiving should be expressed *regardless*. Not until we learn to give thanks *in everything* will we discover God's most basic lessons for our lives—even in times of distress—even in times of sorrow and grief.

EFLECTIONS ON SORROW AND GRIEF

1. Have you or a close friend of yours recently traveled through the deep dark vale of sorrow and grief? If so, there is a fragility and tenderness in your life that such experiences bring about. Answer several questions:

   a. Have you fully expressed your grief?
      (Don't hurry . . . try not to deny its depths.)
   b. Are you being honest about your feelings?
      (It is easy to put up a false front of strength.)
   c. Do you still entertain some anger . . . maybe even feelings of cynicism?
      (Take another look at the psalmist's words in verse 11.)
   d. Can you bring yourself to admit your need for others?
      (They are there . . . awaiting your invitation.)

2. How long has it been since you literally made a list of the Lord's benefits? Start with a clean sheet of paper, address it to the Lord your God, and as Elizabeth Barrett Browning once did, begin with these words at the top: "How do I love thee? Let me count the ways. . . ." Then list fifteen to twenty of His benefits. Psalm 103 will help get your list started.

3. A vow, as we were reminded in the song, is a serious thing. Think back over the vows of your life . . . those times when you made promises to the Lord, either publicly or privately. Have you kept them? Do you need to return and come to terms with one or two? Do that this week.

PSALM

Aleph.

How blessed are those whose
way is blameless,
Who walk in the law of the
Lord.
How blessed are those who observe His
testimonies,
Who seek Him with all their heart.
They also do no unrighteousness;
They walk in His ways.
Thou hast ordained Thy precepts,
That we should keep them diligently.
Oh that my ways may be established
To keep Thy statutes!
Then I shall not be ashamed
When I look upon all Thy
commandments.
I shall give thanks to Thee with
uprightness of heart,
When I learn Thy righteous judgments.
I shall keep Thy statutes;
Do not forsake me utterly!   [119:1–8]

Mem.

O how I love Thy law!
It is my meditation all the day.
Thy commandments make me wiser than
my enemies,
For they are ever mine.
I have more insight than all my teachers,
For Thy testimonies are my meditation.
I understand more than the aged,
Because I have observed Thy
precepts.   [119:97–100]

THE GRIND OF
LOW ENTHUSIASM

Interesting word, enthusiasm. It is from two Greek terms, *en* (meaning "in") and *theos* (meaning "God")—in other words, enthusiasm represents the presence of God in one's life. That makes sense. The truth of God applied to our circumstances brings a burst of enthusiasm nothing else can provide.

New homes, boats, cars, and clothes give us a temporary "high"—until the payments grind on. A new job is exciting, but that dries up in a few months. A new marriage partner makes us feel "up" until reality begins to erase the fun memories of a fantasy honeymoon. All those things may eventually leave us feeling responsible or disappointed or disillusioned . . . sometimes even a little bored. But not when we put "God in"?

Psalm 119—the longest song in the ancient hymnal—is a song that is full of "God in" kind of statements. Over and over it affirms the value of having God's Word in our lives. It keeps pounding away on that theme with a heavy, powerful beat to the music. There is one statement after another announcing the joys, the fresh motivation, the unique benefits of God's Book in our lives. Let's get a grasp of the whole song before we concentrate our attention on a few select stanzas.

OVERVIEW

Length

As I have mentioned, this is the longest song. Not only that, it is the longest chapter in the whole Bible—176 verses. No other chapter even comes close in length.

Structure

Find a Bible and locate Psalm 119. You will notice that the verses of this lengthy song are divided into twenty-two sections, eight verses each. Each section has a title, such as "Aleph," "Beth," "Gimel," etc. These words are really not words at all, but the letters that comprise the Hebrew alphabet. There are twenty-two letters in all, which explains the song's composition in twenty-two sections. Every section of this ancient hymn was originally written with each verse in that section beginning with the same Hebrew letter. In other words, all eight verses in the "Aleph" section of the Hebrew Bible, originally began with that same letter—"Aleph." This poetical structure (called "acrostic" or "acronym") greatly eased the discipline of committing the entire psalm to memory.

Theme

As I have implied, the psalm carries as its theme the *Word of God*. I have found only a very few verses that fail to mention the Scriptures. There are several synonyms employed by the composer that refer to the written Scriptures. Some are:

Word	Testimonies
Law	Judgments
Ways	Statutes
Paths	Commandments
Precepts	Ordinances

An old German version of the Bible places the following description at the head of Psalm 119: "This is the Christian's Golden ABCs of the praise, love, power, and use of the Word of God."

Purpose

The psalmist desires to give praise to God for His Word, and then he states how we are to behave in relation to it.

APPLICATION

Many well-meaning folks are seeking what I would call a "spiritual high" . . . sort of an emotional narcotic that will quiet the pain of their aching, monotonous lives. As a result, you will find people driving miles and miles to attend nightly meetings or standing in long lines to experience some high-level delight that will send them back home on the crest of ecstasy. But all this inevitably leads to emotional hangovers. God's Word—His written Truth—provides the Christian with all the nutrients and true enthusiasm he (or she) can absorb. Coupled with the indwelling Holy Spirit's motivating power, God's Word can virtually transform a life *without a single hangover*—guaranteed!

Believers need to get back to the basics! If Psalm 119 says anything, it says we must be willing to sink our shafts down into His Book and stand *alone* on the principles it contains. Pour over it. Pray over it. Read it. Study it. Memorize sections of it. Meditate upon it. Let it saturate your thinking. Use it when problems arise. Filter your decisions through it. Don't let a day pass without spending time alone with God, listening to the silent voice of His eloquent Word.

Please . . . please heed my counsel! All other attempts to gain spiritual growth lead to frustration. I know; I've tried many of them. And with each one my enthusiasm waned; with God's Word it never has! Nothing enables us to live beyond the grind of low enthusiasm like a daily application of His Word to our situation—absolutely nothing!

Look at an example. Turn to Psalm 119:97–100. I want to reinforce my point by considering the songwriter's words regarding the benefits of consistent scriptural input.

> O how I love Thy law!
> It is my meditation all the day.
> Thy commandments make me wiser than my enemies,
> For they are ever mine.
> I have more insight than all my teachers,
> For Thy testimonies are my meditation.
> I understand more than the aged,
> Because I have observed Thy precepts.

He exclaims, "I love your Word!" He declares his affection for what God has said and has allowed to be written and preserved. Nothing on earth compares to the power of God's Word.

I once came across a powerful quote by Daniel Webster that illustrates what the composer is saying here in verse 97. In the presence of Professor Sanborn of Dartmouth College, Mr. Webster laid his hand on a copy of the Scriptures as he said,

> This is THE Book. I have read through the entire Bible many times. I make it a practice to go through it once a year. It is the Book of all others for lawyers as well as divines; and I pity the man who cannot find in it a rich supply of thought and rules for his conduct. It fits man for life; it prepares him for death.[9]

In verses 98–100, the psalmist speaks of the superiority of the Word over three sources of truth held in high esteem by the world.

1. The Word makes us wiser than our enemies.

> Thy commandments make me wiser than my enemies,
> For they are ever mine. [v. 98]

The world places great importance on knowledge gained from *experience*. In this case, the songwriter mentions experience in dealing with our enemies. But he says that the one who has a grasp of the Word is wiser than his enemies. I feel my enthusiasm beginning to grow with that thought.

2. The Word gives us more insight than all our teachers.

> I have more insight than all my teachers,
> For Thy testimonies are my meditation. [v. 99]

The world also emphasizes the importance of getting knowledge from *education*. But the Lord says that the one who knows the Word possesses more insight than his educators. My enthusiasm is increasing.

3. The Word causes us to have more understanding than the aged.

> I understand more than the aged,
> Because I have observed Thy precepts. [v. 100]

The world embraces enormous respect for *old age* . . . claiming that age equals understanding. But verse 100 declares that one who obeys God's Word can actually have more understanding than an aged individual. In Job 32:8–9, we find a similar observation: "But it is a spirit in man, / And the breath of the Almighty gives them understanding. / The abundant in years may not be wise, / Nor may elders understand justice."

What have we found? We have found that a knowledge and application of the written truths of the Word will better equip us for life than our experiences, our teachers, and even the aged! High-level enthusiasm grips me!

I notice something else. Glance over verses 98–100 again. Three things become a reality in the lives and thinking of those who absorb the Word: wisdom, insight, and understanding.

To illustrate the meaning and distinction of each, I will use a simple diagram:

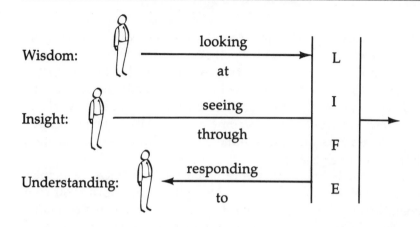

Wisdom, as we learned previously, means the ability to *look at* life and its difficulties from God's point of view. As I learn more of the Word of God and begin to get a grasp of its practical principles, I also glean the ability to look at life from God's viewpoint. I begin to see my circumstances as opportunities He has designed to develop me and train me as His vessel. This removes bitterness and irritation from my life and replaces them with gratitude and enthusiasm!

Insight means the ability to *see through* life and its difficulties from God's viewpoint. In other words, as I grow in the Word, I gain the ability to penetrate beyond the *surface level* of irritations and problems. I am given insight to see the real causes for certain situations, much like God can see beneath the outer mask (1 Sam. 16:7). Make no mistake about it, teachers can communicate knowledge, but the Word alone can give you insight.

Understanding means the ability to *respond to* life's situations/difficulties from God's viewpoint. As I get a hold on the Word, I discover how to react when things don't turn out my way. I find that my attitude is as important to God as my activity . . . often more so!

Before we end this study and take up a new one, let's set these three realities in concrete by looking at a problem from life.

Let's imagine that you recently got a job that has proven to be less than you expected. You prayed for employment, then, lo and behold, this job opened up. You were grateful. After a few weeks, however, you have found that the working conditions leave much to be desired. Furthermore, the fellow employees are all non-Christian and petty. Your first and *natural* response would be disappointment, perhaps even disillusionment. This would lead to daily irritations and possible arguments with others. Your life would soon become a whole pile of negative, pessimistic assaults on others—maybe even God. Exit: motivation. Enter: low enthusiasm.

How much better to apply some basic, biblical principles! Let's say that you were now getting into the Word. You soon come across the fact that God is working on you personally. You are His personal "project." His plan is to develop you into a mature, stable person. He has your good at heart. Nothing is "coincidental" in the Christian life . . . all things (even your job!) work together for good.

Suddenly, it dawns upon you that your job, with all its limitations and irritations, is a perfect place for God to mature you and make you patient. You begin to anticipate each day as another opportunity to grow in grace toward others and submission to Him. Wisdom helps you look at your situation from His viewpoint.

Then, those who work around you don't bother you so much because God's Word has begun to teach you how to see through their surface problems. You now see that their verbal assaults are indicative of a deeper problem of inner unrest. You also learn that you need not take their abuse personally, for it really isn't directed at you personally. Almost overnight, your *insight* has saved you from an ugly, irritating, retaliatory spirit. Instead of arguing with them, you find that you are interested in *helping* them.

You have now begun to respond to your once-irritating occupation with a positive attitude. Time spent in the Letter of James, for example, has resulted in your being very careful about what you say and how you behave before the lost . . . and in your doing a diligent job regardless of the circumstances. What has happened? You have gleaned *understanding.* Furthermore, you have begun to enjoy and accept the challenge of your situation because you know it is exactly where the Lord wants you. It is an ideal place for making Christ known.

God's Word is for *you*, my friend, not just the theologian or the pastor; it's for you! There is no situation that you cannot face if you are really serious about spending time on a regular basis in the Book of books! And a great place to start is Psalm 119, especially if the grind of low enthusiasm has begun to take its toll.

EFLECTIONS ON LOW ENTHUSIASM

1. On a scale of one to ten, ten being best, how high would you rate your daily level of enthusiasm? A nine? Perhaps five? Would you have to say two? Do you find that your day begins better than it ends? Do you see yourself a victim of circumstances? Are you to the point of wondering if *anyone* could be enthusiastic living with all the stuff you have to put up with? All this week, focus every spare moment you have on Psalm 119. Leave your Bible open to it so you can return to it quickly and easily. As you read, pray. Ask God to bring back a fresh, authentic supply of "God-in" enthusiasm.

2. Remember the imaginary illustration I ended with in the applicational part of this week's reading? It was based on the wisdom, insight, and understanding mentioned in Psalm 119:98–100. Go back and re-read those verses and that closing example. Then, this week, write an *actual* example from your own life. In what way are you finding wisdom, insight, and understanding at work in your life?

3. Tell one other person this weekend about something you learned from reading this song. Explain your project of reading through Psalm 119, then state at least one thing that has brought back some much-needed enthusiasm.

PSALMS

A Song of Ascents, of Solomon

Unless the Lord builds the house,
They labor in vain who build it;
Unless the Lord guards the city,
The watchman keeps awake in
vain.
It is vain for you to rise up early,
To retire late,
To eat the bread of painful labors;
For He gives to His beloved even in his
sleep.

Behold, children are a gift of the Lord;
The fruit of the womb is a reward.
Like arrows in the hand of a warrior.
So are the children of one's youth.
How blessed is the man whose quiver is
full of them;
They shall not be ashamed,
When they speak with their enemies in
the gate.   [127:1–5]

———————

A Song of Ascents

How blessed is everyone who fears the
    Lord,
Who walks in His ways.
When you shall eat of the fruit of your
    hands,
You will be happy and it will be well
    with you.
Your wife shall be like a fruitful vine,
Within your house,
Your children like olive plants
Around your table.
Behold, for thus shall the man be blessed
Who fears the Lord.

The Lord bless you from Zion,
And may you see the prosperity of
    Jerusalem all the days of your life.
Indeed, may you see your children's
    children.
Peace be upon Israel!   [128:1–6]

THE GRIND OF
FAMILY LIFE

Maybe it doesn't sound very spiritual, but some phases of family living can be a grind! Rearing a household of busy children, maintaining good communication, living unselfishly with others day in and day out under the same roof, remaining positive and affirming, dealing with strong wills, and handling some of the other domestic challenges can be a first-class chore! Hats off to all who do their very best. To set the record straight, it is worth all the effort. Someday, parents, those children will "rise up and call you blessed." Don't count on it too soon . . . I said *someday*! I am pleased to discover that the ancient songs in God's eternal hymnal do not omit words of encouragement for families.

Periodically, we come across psalms that fit together, forming a unit or a progression of thought. This is true of Psalms 22, 23, and 24. It is also true of Psalms 90 and 91 as well as Psalms 111 and 112. One psalm sets the stage, we might say, while the next completes the picture.

This is precisely what we find in the two songs we are highlighting this week. Both have to do with life in the *home*. They are domestic psalms. How do we know that? Look at 127:1— it refers to the building of the house. Then 127:3–5 mentions children. The third verse of Psalm 128 pictures the wife, the home, and children again, and Psalm 128:6 even traces the progression of time to one's grandchildren. If you think upon this theme, you also observe the psalmist's idea of national strength being connected to the strong family unit in Psalm 128:5. A nation remains only as strong as her families. A crumbling family life is one of the signs of a crumbling culture.

Evangelist Billy Graham in his book *World Aflame,* writes discerning yet serious words concerning America:

> The immutable law of sowing and reaping has held sway. We are now the hapless possessors of moral depravity, and we seek in vain for a cure. The tares of indulgence have overgrown the wheat of moral restraint. Our homes have suffered. Divorce has grown to epidemic proportions. When the morals of society are upset, the family is the first to suffer. The home is the basic unit of our society, and a nation is only as strong as her homes. The breaking up of a home does not often make headlines, but it eats like termites at the structure of the nation.
>
> As a result of the mounting divorces, separations, and desertions, about twelve million of the forty-five million children in the United States [over one-fourth!] do not live with both parents. A vicious circle is set in motion. As the Bible says: "The Fathers have eaten sour grapes, and the children's teeth are set on edge" (Jer. 31:29).

As we turn to a brief examination of Psalms 127 and 128, therefore, we turn to a most relevant portion of Scripture. In our desperate national need, a return to our Judeo-Christian roots is imperative. For it is these roots that will assist us toward mending the fracture of our domestic bones—the essential skeleton of our great republic.

As I mentioned earlier, these two psalms form a progression. They remind me of a historical mural that wraps its way around a room, depicting a progressive story. The progression carries us from the inception of a home all the way through to the blessings of later years. Let me suggest a simple outline:

    I. Inception of the Home (127:1–2)
   II. Children Born within the Home (127:3–5)
  III. Training of the Children in the Home (128:1–3)
  IV. Blessings of Later Years beyond the Home (128:4–6)

I would urge you to pause right now and read both of the psalms again with this outline in mind.

Now then, let's see how it ties together.

INCEPTION OF THE HOME

Unless the Lord builds the house,
They labor in vain who build it;
Unless the Lord guards the city,
The watchman keeps awake in vain.
It is vain for you to rise up early,
To retire late,
To eat the bread of painful labors;
For He gives to His beloved even in his sleep. [127:1–2]

There are two major ideas conveyed in these two verses:

1. The Lord Himself is to be the center of our home (v. 1). There is an emphatic repetition of the phrase, "unless the Lord. . . ." As in the English, it is an *identical* repetition in the Hebrew Bible. What's more, it appears first in each sentence, adding even more emphasis to the thought. Of course, the idea is not that the Lord uses a hammer and nails so that He can literally "build the house," nor that He holds a weapon that He might literally "guard the city." The meaning is that He must be the very Foundation upon which a home is built before that home will stand firm. He must be the unseen Guardian of a city, trusted completely, before a city can be considered safe.

If such is not the case, all is "in vain" (also mentioned twice). In fact, in the Hebrew sentence structure, the words *in vain* appear first in each clause, emphasizing the emptiness of it all:

". . . *in vain* they labor who build it."

". . . *in vain* the watchman keeps awake."

Work, strive, fret, worry, plan, strain all you wish, but if the Lord is not the very *center* of your home, all your additional effort to make it strong is futile and worthless, Mom and Dad.

2. The Lord Himself must be the center of our life and work (v. 2). In keeping with the context of these two songs, verse 2

has reference to making a living—working long and hard hours. His point is that long, hard hours *by themselves* will never result in a godly, happy home—only "painful labors." And please note that if the Lord is *first* in our lives, He will reward us even in our sleep. A godly life includes times of rest and relaxation.

There is an ancient Greek motto that I learned many years ago. It says: "You will break the bow if you keep it always bent." That is worth some thought. Do I write to a parent who has become too busy, too hurried, too stressed out? God says He will reward you even in your sleep! Though you may feel too involved to back off and rest, you'd better! And on the other hand, if the Lord is not the very nucleus of your life, all the labor of a lifetime cannot serve as a substitute for Him. Long hours and painful labors, rising early and retiring late can never replace your allegiance to the Lord and His presence in your home. Money cannot replace Christ! Neither can things, or promises that circumstances will change "someday."

So let's get this straight, right at the foundation level of instruction on a happy home: *Christ must be first.* You must be a believer in the Lord Jesus Christ and you must marry one who is a believer if you wish to establish your home with full strength and stability . . . also if you hope to tap into the potential power for living victoriously.

CHILDREN BORN WITHIN THE HOME

Behold, children are a gift of the Lord;
The fruit of the womb is a reward.
Like arrows in the hand of a warrior.
So are the children of one's youth.
How blessed is the man whose quiver is full of them;
They shall not be ashamed,
When they speak with their enemies in the gate. [127:3–5]

The songwriter grabs our attention with "Behold!" He says, in effect, "Pay attention . . . listen up!" These three verses take us a step further as they address the coming of children into the home, and the parents' proper attitude toward such.

Notice three titles the songwriter gives to children: (1) "gift," (2) "reward," and (3) "arrows." Each one calls for some analysis.

The term *gift* is a translation of the Hebrew word that means "property, possession . . . that which is shared/assigned." Children are the Lord's possessions and the property, which He graciously assigns to or shares with parents. Now this third verse doesn't say "some children" or even "most children," but simply "children," implying *all* children . . . *your* children! There is no such thing as an "accidental birth" or a "surprise pregnancy" from God's viewpoint. And wise are the parents who acknowledge the fact that their child is a personal gift from God. If you and I truly believe that each child is "assigned" by God, what a difference it can make with the child *we* may not have planned!

The word *reward* conveys the idea of pleasure—something given as a tangible proof of appreciation. Children are never to be viewed as punishment for God's displeasure—quite the contrary! The fruit of the womb is God's very personal trophy of His love, His choice reward.

The word *arrow* is equally meaningful. You'll notice that the word picture is that of a warrior with arrows in his hand. Imagine the scene. A warrior in battle doesn't stop to *make* his arrows, nor does he *ignore* them. He *uses* them. He *directs* them toward a target. A parent is responsible for the *direction* of his children. A child, like an arrow, is incapable of directing himself. It is the basic responsibility of parents to direct the early lives of their children. This makes a great deal of sense when you consider that a child is born in a state of depravity and inner sinfulness. You must stop here and read Psalm 51:5 along with Psalm 58:3. Both verses verify that children are born in a state of iniquity. Solomon's saying in Proverbs 22:15 underscores this fact: "Foolishness is bound up in the heart of a child; / The rod of discipline will remove it far from him." Children need parental authority.

What happens when a child isn't given direction? Let's allow Proverbs 29:15 to answer that question:

The rod and reproof give wisdom,
But a child who gets his own way brings shame to his mother.

A more literal translation of the verse would be, ". . . but a child left, brings shame to his mother." Left alone in his room to play? No. The thought is of a child left in the original condition in which he is born; a child who is not given direction will bring shame to his mother. Look at Proverbs 22:6 for a moment:

> Train up a child in the way he should go,
> Even when he is old he will not depart from it.

Without question, this is one of the most familiar verses in Proverbs, but how seldom it is correctly understood. The words *train up* come from the Hebrew term *kake,* meaning "palate, roof of the mouth, gums." The verbal form of this term was used to describe two different actions in two unrelated realms:

1. Newborn infants. The midwife in ancient times would take a newborn child into her arms, dip her finger in the juice of crushed dates, grapes, or olive oil and then reach inside the mouth of the infant and rub its palate or gums, causing the baby to suck as the flavor was tasted. In other words, she would *create a thirst* for the mother's milk. Then the infant would be placed on the mother's breast for nourishment.

2. Young horses. When a horse was wild, a rope was placed in its mouth as a bridle, and it was ridden until it became "broken" and submissive. In other words, the *self-will was broken* in the horse.

Both aptly describe what is involved in "training up" a child. It includes creating a thirst for the spiritual life. It also includes breaking the stubborn self-will and replacing it with a gentle, tender, submissive spirit.

Next, please observe that the parent is to do these things according to the child's way. The Amplified Bible helps capture the full meaning of the original Hebrew as it renders this portion of Proverbs 22:6 with the paraphrase: "in keeping with his individual gift or bent." In other words, the training administered by the parents is to be unique with each offspring. The parent, therefore, must know his child, must understand the "bent" of each one of his children and adapt his training for each according to that "bent." How does a parent come to know the bent of each child? According to Proverbs 20:11–12:

> It is by his deeds that a lad distinguishes himself
> If his conduct is pure and right.
> The hearing ear and the seeing eye,
> The Lord has made both of them.

Parents, we are responsible for listening to and looking at our children. Let's open our ears! Let's open our eyes! Think! Observe! We will never fulfill our part of Proverbs 22:6 correctly until we really come to *know each of our children*. God has given each child a unique makeup, a series of strengths and weaknesses. The wise parent learns the inward pattern of each child and fits his (or her) training to the need. How foolish to think that all kids are the same. They're not. Nor will they be directed correctly if the parent blindly and brutally disciplines without knowledge. We are to train each child according to "his way."

In case you think that all children in the same family have the same "bent," study Cain and Abel, Jacob and Esau, Absalom and Solomon, Isaac and Ishmael, and the children in *your own* family. According to Psalm 139:13–16, each child is uniquely planned and put together by God in the mother's womb. Wise are the parents who make a study of each one of the children born to them.

These are not new and novel thoughts on child-rearing. This process is explained in great detail in chapter 5 of my book *Growing Wise in Family Life*.[10]

Each child is to be viewed as a gift, a reward, and an arrow in our hands. Verse 5 of Psalm 127 says that we are to be happy when we have all the "arrows" God has designed for our quivers. And let me add a final thought: Not everyone has the same size quiver! The same Lord who gives fruit to the womb determines the size of each family quiver.

Perhaps you are fretting and chafing under the size of your quiver today. This is not what God desires. He wants you to be satisfied and happy, not frustrated and irritable. There is no joy like the joy that comes from God-given arrows in our divinely determined quivers.

TRAINING OF THE CHILDREN IN THE HOME

How blessed is everyone who fears the Lord,
Who walks in His ways.
When you shall eat of the fruit of your hands,
You will be happy and it will be well with you.
Your wife shall be like a fruitful vine,
Within your house,
Your children like olive plants
Around your table. [Ps. 128:1–3]

In Psalm 127 the arrows are in our hands, needing direction. As the songwriter continues his thoughts regarding the family in Psalm 128, he says that "everyone who fears the Lord" will be blessed or happy. The context is *the family*, remember—specifically, the children God gives. As the progression continues in Psalm 128:1–2, we see how each arrow is to be carefully directed: (1) in the fear of the Lord, and (2) walking in His ways. Again, you will notice, happiness will continue to be the surrounding atmosphere ("how blessed").

Parents who train their children according to biblical principles have the hope of ultimate happiness. As a matter of fact, verse 2 says your investment will allow you to "eat of the fruit of your hands" and "it will be well with you." The picture is, again, the hands (as it was in 127:4). Parents' hands enjoy the product of their labor as they "pick the fruit" of the domestic garden they have cultivated. As submission is caught, obedience taught, and understanding sought, the dividends come rolling in!

Verse 3 is such a pleasant picture. The father looks around the supper table. He sees his dear wife ("a fruitful vine") and children ("olive plants"). I notice that the children are not called "branches" but plants. This seems to emphasize that each offspring is independent, unique, one who will reproduce his own kind in later years. And the difference is also seen in that the mother is pictured as *a vine*, but the children as *olive plants*. This is a good and necessary distinction.

We, as parents, are unwise to assume that our children are put together exactly like we are. The father, for example, who is athletic, has a strong tendency to want that same tendency to emerge in his son, even to the point of forcing it. The same is true of a mother who is artistic. She persistently urges that talent in her daughter, but frequently that isn't the daughter's interest. Why? To answer with the songwriter's symbols: we are *vines*, but our children are *olive plants*. However, regardless of a child's talent (or lack of it), athletic ability (or lack of it), the training we give him or her must be that of *spiritual instruction* ("fear of the Lord"). A child *must be directed toward faith in the Lord Jesus Christ* and given an enormous amount of training in the principles of Scripture.

On occasion I have heard well-meaning young couples say that they are going to "let the children choose for themselves" when it comes to their spiritual lives. For fear of "warping their children" and "making fanatics out of them," some parents take a hands-off policy—an unfortunate mistake. As soon as the child's independent self-will emerges, he or she (dominated by a sinful nature) chooses to ignore the Lord, the local church, the instruction of the Scriptures, and the godly life. Remember, Solomon's warning? He declared that "Foolishness is bound up in the heart of a child" (Prov. 22:15). And also, as we saw earlier, David tells us that depravity—that inward undertow of evil—is part of the makeup of every child. My point is that a young child *cannot* "make up his own mind" correctly. His inner nature counteracts and overpowers godliness. Now I certainly do not believe in fanaticism. That is not our goal; but a balanced, victorious, growing spiritual life *is*. Without direction, a child will seldom (if ever) choose the path of obedience on his own.

If you think the grind of family life is a tough challenge, try to imagine the attitudes and atmosphere in your home if each child were told to just make up his (or her) own mind. The grind would become so severe, no one could endure the pressure!

LATER YEARS IN THE HOME

Behold, for thus shall the man be blessed
Who fears the Lord.

The Lord bless you from Zion,
And may you see the prosperity of Jerusalem all the days of your
  life.
Indeed, may you see your children's children.
Peace be upon Israel! [Ps. 128:4–6]

The domestic scene now reaches completion. The children are trained, raised, and launched from the nest. The psalmist paints a pleasant picture of serenity. In doing so, he mentions three realms of blessing:

1. Personal pleasure (v. 4). The psalmist says "for thus" happiness comes. For what? For all the hard work and consistent training invested by parents, happiness comes as God's reward. Believe me, if you determine to have Christ as the central figure of your home and His Word as the authority in rearing your children, you have your work cut out for you!

You will find that you'll be outnumbered, scoffed, considered strange by your neighbors (and a few teachers), criticized, misunderstood, and tempted to compromise. The very forces of hell will unleash their fury on you! You will be on your knees and in the Word regularly. But, if you maintain the standard (with love, gentleness, and consistency), God promises that you will look back in your twilight years and enjoy inward, personal pleasure. The converse is also true. If you relinquish your responsibilities as a parent, you can expect sad and serious consequences.

2. Civic benefits (v. 5). Even Zion will be blessed! Jerusalem will be prosperous and strong! The point is this: Your offspring will be used to make a dent in society—for good! All the days of your later life, you'll enjoy the fact that your earlier direction and private contribution to the home life of your children pay off in rich, public dividends.

3. National blessings (v. 6). Now, in this final verse, grandchildren arrive on the scene. You, the grandparent, see them,

and you witness a second-generation investment. Your own children pass on similar training so that the entire nation benefits and is blessed because the Lord, originally, was at the very center of your home.

CONCLUSION

Psalms 127 and 128 will not soon be forgotten, will they? They have encouraged us to establish the right foundation for our homes: the Lord Jesus Christ. They have instructed us to look upon the family as a God-given responsibility. We have been admonished to direct our offspring God's way, according to *His* prescribed plan. Finally, we have been promised personal, civic, and national blessings as a result of our efforts. If we apply these truths as God has spoken, the grind of family life will be greatly reduced. You can count on it!

I recently came across an anonymous piece that portrays the family as a garden. It suggests various things we can plant in our family relationships that will result in great benefits:

A family is like many things, perhaps most like a garden. It needs time, attention, and cultivation. The sunshine of laughter and affirmation. It also needs the rains of difficulties, tense moments, serious discussions about issues that matter. And there must be spade work, where hardness is broken loose and planting of fresh seeds is accomplished with lots of TLC. Here are some suggestions for fifteen rows worth planting:

Plant four rows of peas:	Preparedness
	Perseverance
	Promptness
	Politeness
Then three rows of squash:	Squash gossip
	Squash criticism
	Squash indifference

Along with five rows
   of lettuce: Let us be faithful
                                               Let us be unselfish
                                               Let us be loyal
                                               Let us love one another
                                               Let us be truthful

And three rows of turnips: Turn up with a smile
                                               Turn up with a new idea
                                               Turn up with determination

And then? Well, from then on it's pretty simple. Water, weed, tend with care, and patiently watch the garden grow. Someday you'll look back and realize it was worth all the years of all the work and effort and prayer. Like a lovely garden, your family will be a thing of grateful pride, of seasonal beauty, of daily sustenance.

REFLECTIONS ON FAMILY LIFE

1. Biblical instruction on the family is always insightful. That shouldn't surprise us, since God holds the patent on marriage and the establishment of a home. In light of that, return to Genesis in your Bible and read again the passages of primary reference on this subject. Take your time! Read Genesis 1:26–31 and 2:18–25. What stands out as *most* significant?

2. Think back to your original home—the place you were raised, the family unit from which you came. Ponder some positive scenes that are still vivid in your memory . . . a time when you (a) felt secure, (b) were affirmed, (c) learned a valuable—maybe painful—lesson, and (4) your whole family pulled together during a crisis. Do you still have a parent, a brother, or sister living? Give one a call (or write) and "relive" one of those scenes. Express your love. Explain what led you to contact him (or her).

3. Perhaps the most encouraging thought from our study of these two songs is that we are rearing our nation's future (128:5–6). Take some one-on-one time this week with each of your children and talk about the importance of this in tomorrow's world. Get specific. Include a few hugs of affirmation. Don't be afraid to include those great words . . . not just "Love ya!" but "I love you!" Finally, work hard to cultivate all those fifteen rows of very special plants. Someday, you'll be glad you did.

PSALM

A Song of Ascents

O Lord, my heart is not proud,
  nor my eyes haughty;
Nor do I involve myself in
  great matters,
Or in things too difficult for me.
Surely I have composed and quieted my
  soul;
Like a weaned child rests against his
  mother,
My soul is like a weaned child within me.
O Israel, hope in the Lord
From this time forth and
  forever.   [131:1–3]

THE GRIND OF IMPATIENT ARROGANCE

Psalm 131 is one of the shortest chapters in the Bible—only three verses in length. If it is ever true, however, that good things come in small packages, this psalm is proof of that. Charles Haddon Spurgeon, that prince of preachers, said of Psalm 131:

> Comparing all the psalms to gems, we should liken this to a pearl; how beautifully it will adorn the neck of patience. . . . ![11]

He aptly describes this little psalm. It would be missed by the hurried reader and considered of almost insignificant value to one impressed with size and choice of terms, but it nevertheless contains a timely message.

David composes lyrics that address a hazardous and dangerous habit in this song: *impatient arrogance.* He is saying that he is not proud or haughty or interested in being seen, heard, or noticed. In fact, he is announcing his plan to move out of the limelight and away from that place of public attention.

Genuine humility isn't something we can announce very easily. To claim this virtue is, as a rule, to forfeit it. Humility is the fairest and rarest flower that blooms. Put it on display and instantly it wilts and loses its fragrance! Humility is one character trait that should be a "closet utterance," as W. Graham Scroggie puts it,[12] not something we announce from the housetop.

Perhaps you have already heard the humorous account of the

fellow who attempted to write about his own humility and had trouble choosing a title for his book. *Humility and How I Attained It* seemed inappropriate, as did *How I Became Very Humble.* He finally decided on *Me and My Humility*—and he inserted twelve full-page pictures of himself!

No, humility is not something to be announced. It simply belongs in one's life, in the private journal of one's walk with God, not in a book that looks like a testimony but comes across more like a "bragimony."

David, however, isn't bragging in Psalm 131. In fact, I don't think David had any idea that his meditations would ever be published and preserved down through the centuries for the world to read. He writes his song exclusively to the Lord (v. 1) and briefly states his convictions concerning his removal from the public eye.

We know nothing of what prompted the writing of this song. As we have already observed, the occasion leading to the writing of many of the ancient biblical songs remains a mystery. We can enter into the occasion in our imagination, however. Often we feel humbled and crushed after we have sinned and/or made a series of mistakes—after we have "blown it." At those times we are genuinely interested in finding the nearest cave and crawling in. At other times when we get a glimpse of our own pride and become sick of our deceptive attempts to cover it up, we fall before God and ask to be removed and made obscure. And then there are those occasions of heart-searching experiences: Times of sickness. Days of deep hurt. Painful waiting. Disappointing events. Loss of a loved one. Removal of a friend. Loneliness. Pressure. At those crossroads, the traffic of people seems overbearing, the flashing of lights seems so vain, and the noisy crowd, so repulsive. During such times one longs for obscurity and silence, humble communion with his Creator. Any of these occasions could have prodded the sweet singer of Israel to write this song of humility:

O Lord, my heart is not proud, nor my eyes haughty;
Nor do I involve myself in great matters,
Or in things too difficult for me.

> Surely I have composed and quieted my soul;
> Like a weaned child rests against his mother,
> My soul is like a weaned child within me.
> O Israel, hope in the Lord
> From this time forth and forever. [131:1–3]

In a matter-of-fact fashion, David addresses the Lord. Throughout the psalm he carries on a conversation with his God. Eight times in the first two verses he uses "I," "me," and "my." This, as we have said, is a page from his own journal.

Verse 1

> O Lord, my heart is not proud, or my eyes haughty;
> Nor do I involve myself in great matters,
> Or in things too difficult for me.

You may remember that in the Hebrew Bible whatever appears *first* in a clause or sentence is frequently placed in that position for the purpose of *emphasis*. This is especially true when the phrase is rearranged and written in an awkward, strange manner. This is precisely what we find in verse 1.

There are three negatives set forth at the very beginning of three clauses: "Not proud" . . . "Not haughty" . . . "Nor do I involve myself." David is communicating the depth of his feelings. The structure of his words reveals strong passion. The terms do, too.

The term *proud* comes from *gah-bah,* meaning "to be high, exalted." He mentions his *heart* first—the root source of pride down deep within. He says that as deeply as God may wish to probe, He will not find a trace of a "high, exalted" attitude within him. God may "search" and "know my heart" (Ps. 139:23) all He wishes, declares David.

The term *haughty* comes from another word having a similar meaning—*room.* This Hebrew term means "to be lifted up, raised." The idea is that one who is proud within shows it in his *eyes,* which are "lifted up, raised." That is exactly what Proverbs 30:11–13 says:

> There is a kind of man who curses his father,
> And does not bless his mother.
> There is a kind who is pure in his own eyes,
> Yet is not washed from his filthiness.
> There is a kind—oh how lofty are his eyes!
> And his eyelids are raised in arrogance.

The "proud look" has to do with eyes that are "lifted up." We have all seen this among the pseudo-sophisticates and on the plastic masks worn by many of the Hollywood stars and television celebrities. David declares that both his heart and his eyes will stand the test of God's scrutiny.

There are two simple and quick ways God says the true condition of the heart is revealed. (Many of us may *think* we can hide it, but we cannot.) The first is through the eyes (as we have seen here) and the second is through the mouth (as Jesus says in Luke 6:45). Of course, one's life is another proof of one's heart condition, but that takes longer to observe. Keen counselors and wise people are careful to listen to words (what is said as well as what *isn't* said) and watch the eyes of others. You soon discover that the heart is like a well and the eyes and tongue are like buckets which draw water from the same well. If true humility is not in the heart, the eyes will show it.

David goes on to say that he does not involve himself in great matters nor difficult things. The idea here is that he doesn't pursue places of prominence or greatness. The simple fact is he doesn't *need* such a place in his life any longer. He is not only willing but pleased to be removed from the public platform of fickle applause.

This reminds me of another great man of God—Moses. According to Acts 7:22, he was educated in the finest schools Egypt had to offer. He was gifted with a powerful personality. He was a most impressive man. He was a mighty warrior—brave, brilliant, and even heroic. It was clear to many that he was destined to be the Pharaoh of the land. At age forty he killed an Egyptian and attempted to deliver his people (the Jews) by his own, powerful arm. Exodus 2:11–15 tells the whole story. This resulted in his fleeing Egypt and winding up in the Midian Desert . . . a hot, dry, forgotten place of obscurity, where he lived for another forty years—unknown and unapplauded. Think of it! Moses—a prominent member of the royal family—spending his days on the parched sands of a desert, suddenly and totally removed from people: shelved, sidelined, and silent. F. B. Meyer writes of this experience:

> But Moses was out of touch with God (in Egypt). So he fled, and crossed the desert that lay between him and the eastern frontier; threaded the mountain passes of the Sinaitic peninsula, through which in after years he was to lead his people; and at last sat wearily down by a well in the land of Midian. . . . and finally to the quiet life of a shepherd in the calm open spaces of that wonderful land, which, on more than one occasion, has served for a Divine school.
>
> Such experiences come to us all. We rush forward, thinking to carry all before us; we strike a few blows in vain; we are staggered with disappointment, and reel back; we are afraid at the first breath of human disapprobation; we flee from the scenes of our discomfiture to hide ourselves in chagrin. Then we are hidden in the secret of God's presence from the pride of man. And there our vision clears: the silt drops from the current of our life, as from the Rhone in its passage through the deep waters of Geneva's lake; our self-life dies down; our spirit drinks of the river of God, which is full of water; our faith begins to grasp his arm, and to be the channel for the manifestation of his power; and thus at last we emerge to be his hand to lead an Exodus.[13]

David, like Moses, chose to slip away and not involve himself in matters of greatness and public glamour. His, for a time at least, was to be a life of solitude and meditation.

Verse 2

How did David respond to this parenthesis of quietness, this back-row seat in the balcony? Was that capable and passionate man of war irritated and out of sorts because he had been reduced from captain of the team to spectator? Not in the least. Listen to verse 2 of Psalm 131:

> Surely I have composed and quieted my soul;
> Like a weaned child rests against his mother,
> My soul is like a weaned child within me.

There is not the slightest irritation in his words. The term *composed* means "to be smooth, even, level." The same Hebrew word used here also appears in Isaiah 28:25 with reference to a farmer's field that had once been rough and rugged but was now planted and "level." David is saying that his inner soul is not churning and stormy, but is calm and smooth. It is a beautiful description of tranquility and patience. The result is that he is "quieted" within; he is inwardly silent and still. He is like the words of the hymn by Jean Pigott that Hudson Taylor loved to sing while reaching the lost in inland China:

> Jesus, I am resting, resting
> In the joy of what Thou art;
> I am finding out the greatness
> Of Thy loving heart. . . .

Or perhaps more like the beloved Scandinavian hymn by Katharina von Schlegel:

> Be still, my soul! the Lord is on thy side;
> Bear patiently the cross of grief or pain;
> Leave to thy God to order and provide;
> In every change He faithful will remain.
> Be still, my soul! thy best, thy heavenly Friend
> Thro' thorny ways leads to a joyful end.

After the statement declaring his inner calm condition, David gives a tender illustration of a baby quietly resting on its mother—and twice he uses the word *weaned* to describe the child. The little tot is no longer striving and fretting with his mother for her milk . . . no longer demanding nor restless. All is calm. The roughness of self-will has been smoothed and is now calm and contented.

But wait! This isn't complete unless you see how the symbolic analogy fits into David's experience. Let's do that by answering three questions:

1. Who is the child? It is David's inward being.

2. Who is the mother? It is his public life . . . the familiar applause of people.

3. From what is it weaned? Clearly, it means he is weaned from the desire for prominence, the place of honor—the limelight. "I no longer need that," says David. "I'm weaned!"

Verse 3

> O Israel, hope in the Lord
> From this time forth and forever.

As is true of all of us on special occasions, David had learned a truth that was so exciting he *had* to share it. He wanted his entire nation to enter into this joyous experience with him.

Please allow me a personal comment here. David's little song has been so comforting to me. I have loved its quiet peacefulness. I have needed its message. Perhaps you have, too. It is quite possible that God is "weaning" you away from every source of pride. You may have trusted in the fleeting silver and tinsel of this world, only to have it tarnish and melt in your hands. You may have believed in someone only to have him (or her) fail you and even turn against you. You, quite possibly, have fallen into the trap of self-exaltation and recently failed miserably. Maybe you've been accustomed to honor and public notice, but (like Moses) all that has passed, at least for a while. Perhaps your talent is no longer in demand . . . or your job is not now needed . . . or your counsel is no longer sought. "What's happening?" you may be asking. Arrogance refuses to accept such blows, but patience overrules and stills our souls at such times. But "Why?" you may wonder. God is answering your question in Psalm 131. You are being "weaned" from the mother of importance, prestige, public applause, honor . . . and (dare I say it?) *pride.*

Who does the weaning? The child? No, never. The act of weaning is done *to* the child, not *by* it. *God is responsible.* He is removing every crutch upon which you would lean . . . every crutch but Himself . . . so you will lean hard upon *Him* only, as Proverbs 3:5–6 says so beautifully. He is changing your diet to a new kind of food—from the milk of immaturity to the meat of genuine humility. And He wants you to learn this "from this time forth and forever."

 EFLECTIONS
ON IMPATIENT
ARROGANCE

1. Give your own definitions:

   Arrogance: _____

   _____

   Impatience: _____

   _____

   Quiet composure: _____

   _____

   Humility: _____

   _____

2. Take time to analyze how you are put together. Do you *have* to be in the center of attention in order to feel ful-filled? Why? Why not? Would others think of you as self-assured and confident . . . or arrogant? Why? Why not? One more: If you were suddenly sidelined by a serious accident or illness which removed you from the fast lane of activity, could you handle that without a great deal of adjustment? Why? Why not?

3. Can you think of someone you admire for his or her gen-uine humility? Isn't it remarkable how Christlike such a trait is? Go to the trouble of making a creative thank-you card that illustrates and expresses your gratitude . . . and see that the card gets into his (or her) hands *anonymously*. State in a few words (maybe your own poem?) your appre-ciation, but leave it unsigned.

PSALM

By the rivers of Babylon,
There we sat down and wept,
When we remembered Zion.
Upon the willows in the midst
  of it
We hung our harps.
For there our captors demanded of us
  songs,
And our tormentors mirth, saying,
"Sing us one of the songs of Zion."

How can we sing the Lord's song
In a foreign land?
If I forget you, O Jerusalem,
May my right hand forget her skill.
May my tongue cleave to the roof of my
  mouth,
If I do not remember you,
If I do not exalt Jerusalem
Above my chief joy.

Remember, O Lord, against the sons of
  Edom
The day of Jerusalem,
Who said, "Raze it, raze it,
To its very foundation."
O daughter of Babylon, you devastated
  one,
How blessed will be the one who repays
  you
With the recompense with which you
  have repaid us.
How blessed will be the one who seizes
  and dashes your little ones
Against the rock.   [137:1–9]

THE GRIND OF LINGERING CONSEQUENCES

No one can deny the relentless pain brought on by enduring the consequences of wrong actions. It may be as quick and simple as the sting following a swat from a parent's paddle or as lingering and severe as a prison sentence. Either one, however, is hard to bear. "The way of transgressors is hard" (Prov. 13:15, KJV).

The person who cheats on a mate and later leaves the marriage must ultimately endure the consequences. The child who runs away from home in a fit of rebellious rage must live with the painful ramifications. The politician who assures his voters of unrealistic and unachievable promises if elected must face his critics after election. The minister who compromises in the realm of ethics or morals must live with the private shame and loss of public respect. The list goes on and on.

Even though our day is characterized by an erosion of personal responsibility and attempts to soft-pedal or cover up the consequences of wrong, those very difficult days in the backwash of disobedience are nevertheless haunting realities. Sin still bears bitter fruit. Devastating consequences still await the transgressor. "Be not deceived . . . whatsoever a man soweth, that shall he also reap" (Gal. 6:7, KJV) is still in the Book. Few souls live more somber lives in the minor key than those who have disobeyed and must now endure the grind of lingering consequences.

And speaking of a somber, minor key, Psalm 137 comes to mind. Here is a mournful song! The composer is enduring the

pain of past actions that led to his being among a group of captives. As a band of Jewish POWs, they have been taken by the
Babylonians into a foreign land. Immediately, the scene is set:

> By the rivers of Babylon,
> There we sat down and wept,
> When we remembered Zion.

You can skim through the next eight verses and quickly detect other terms that reveal a prisonlike experience:

Verse 3: *our captors . . . our tormentors*
Verse 4: *a foreign land*
Verse 7: *Remember, O Lord, against the sons of Edom*
Verse 8: *O daughter of Babylon, you devastated one*

Why was a Hebrew writer in Babylon? What were the events
that led to his and others' becoming captives of this foreign
power? Believe me, it was no accident. It came to pass exactly as
God had spoken through His prophet Jeremiah:

> Therefore thus says the Lord of hosts, "Because you have not
> obeyed My words, behold, I will send and take all the families of
> the north," declares the Lord, "and I will send to Nebuchadnez-
> zar king of Babylon, My servant, and will bring them against this
> land, and against its inhabitants, and against all these nations
> round about; and I will utterly destroy them, and make them a
> horror, and a hissing, and an everlasting desolation. Moreover, I
> will take from them the voice of joy and the voice of gladness,
> the voice of the bridegroom and the voice of the bride, the sound
> of the millstones and the light of the lamp. And this whole land
> shall be a desolation and a horror, and these nations shall serve
> the king of Babylon seventy years." [Jer. 25:8–11]

Those prophetic warnings were spoken to the people of
Judah. They had persisted in their disobedience for over three
hundred years since the last days of Solomon's reign. The united
kingdom of the Jewish nation had split after Solomon's death. A
civil war followed. Ten of the twelve tribes of Israel settled in

the north under King Jeroboam's leadership. Two settled in the south under King Rehoboam, Solomon's son. The civil war destroyed the Jewish unity and resulted in both groups ultimately falling captive to two foreign Gentile powers.

The northern kingdom is called "Israel" in Scripture and the southern kingdom is called "Judah." Israel had nineteen kings during her two-hundred-plus years before she fell to the Assyrians in 722 B.C. Judah had twenty kings (eight of them were righteous) until the Babylonians (also called Chaldeans) captured them and held them in bondage for seventy years, exactly as Jeremiah predicted. Psalm 137 was written during (or shortly after) Judah's captivity in Babylon.

Now that we have read the song and surveyed its historical background, let's draw an outline from it:

I. Memory of Captivity (vv. 1–3)
 —a personal section—
II. Devotion to the Lord (vv. 4–6)
 —a patriotic section—
III. Plea for Retribution (vv. 7–9)
 —a passionate section—

Few songs in Scripture begin with stronger emotions. The composer is absolutely dejected, feeling awful! He remembers the bitter humiliation, the stinging sarcasm he and his companions had to undergo. He even reminds us of a particular occasion when a representative of Babylon marched those Jews along a river and poked some cynical "fun" at them.

> By the rivers of Babylon,
> There we sat down and wept,
> When we remembered Zion.
> Upon the willows in the midst of it
> We hung our harps.
> For there our captors demanded of us songs,
> And our tormentors mirth, saying,
> "Sing us one of the songs of Zion." [vv. 1–3]

Can't you imagine that scene? With their heads hanging low, their shoulders slumped and tears streaming down their cheeks, those Jewish captives sat silent and gritted their teeth. Talk about a daily grind! This was the pit of pits. I can just hear the taunts of the Babylonian guard as he looked out over those downcast, depressed people of Judah.

"Hey, how about all you Jews joining in on one of those good ol' hymns of the faith! Let's hear it for dear ol' Jehovah! Sing it out, now . . . and as you sing, remember Zion!"

Oh, how that hurt! It hurt so deeply the writer remembered the precise words of his tormentor. This sad scene from Psalm 137 illustrates Galatians 6:7 better than any other Old Testament Scripture. I mentioned it earlier but it bears repeating:

Do not be deceived, God is not mocked; for whatever a man sows, this he will also reap.

The scoffers and critics of Christianity never stand any taller or shout any louder than when God's people publicly fall into sin and are forced to suffer the inevitable consequence. All Satan's hosts dance with glee when believers compromise, play with fire, then get burned. We've seen a lot of that sort of thing in recent years, haven't we? The secular media have a field day as God's people are forced to take it on the chin.

Those captives were getting just what they deserved, and they knew it. There was no more singing, no jokes, and no laughter in that embarrassed Jewish camp on foreign soil. One man describes the scene quite vividly:

This is the bitterest of all—to know that suffering need not have been; that it has resulted from indiscretion and inconsistency; that is the harvest of one's own sowing; that the vulture which feeds on the vitals is a nestling of one's own rearing. Ah me! this is pain! There is an inevitable nemesis in life. The laws of the heart and home, of the soul and human life, cannot be violated with impunity. Sin may be forgiven; the fire of penalty may be changed into the fire of trial; the love of God may seem nearer and dearer than ever and yet there is the awful pressure of pain; the trembling heart; the failing of eyes and pining of soul; the harp on the willows; the refusal to sing the Lord's song. [14]

Do you find yourself on "foreign soil" today? Are you reaping the bitter fruits of carnal sowing? Is your song gone? Are the consequences of your sins pressing upon you? Let me urge you to lay your heart bare before your Lord. Tell Him about it. Be certain that the cause of your dreadful experience is thoroughly confessed . . . and that you are not hiding or denying anything. Once you have claimed your Lord's forgiveness, let me urge you to claim His presence and quietly wait for relief. The consequences of sins—yes, even *forgiven* sins—are often difficult and sometimes lingering. The best way to ride out the storm is *on the rock* (Ps. 40:1–3). A humble and contrite heart is essential before you can expect any relief.

After relating the bitterness of that experience, the writer does a little self-analysis. His emphasis changes from without to within. He asks a very real question in verse 4 of Psalm 137: "How can we sing the Lord's song / In a foreign land?"

That is so true, so *very* true! Genuine singing is spontaneous; it cannot be forced. Nor will it joyfully burst forth from a broken heart or a guilty conscience. It comes as a direct result of the filling of the Holy Spirit, as Paul states in Ephesians 5:18–19:

> And do not get drunk with wine, for that is dissipation, but be filled with the Spirit, speaking to one another in psalms and hymns and spiritual songs, singing and making melody with your heart to the Lord.

In the same stroke of the pen that declares the importance of being Spirit-filled, the apostle Paul also mentions the singing heart.

Did it ever occur to you that just as certain animals cannot reproduce in captivity, neither can the believer? We are totally unable to have Christ's power, victory, and joy reproduced in us while we are still being held captive in the "foreign land" of carnality. Paul and Silas were chained in the Philippian jail, but the Christian melodies and songs rang out nonetheless. Physically and outwardly they were captives, but spiritually and inwardly they were free and full of joy (Acts 16:25–26).

And now in the next three verses of Song 137, with the zeal of a Jewish right-wing patriot, the psalmist states his devotion to his Lord and to the city of his homeland:

> How can we sing the Lord's song
> In a foreign land?
> If I forget you, O Jerusalem,
> May my right hand forget her skill.
> May my tongue cleave to the roof of my mouth,
> If I do not remember you,
> If I do not exalt Jerusalem
> Above my chief joy. [vv. 4–6]

Notice that the subject now changes from "we" and "our" to "I" and "my." He says that he will never, ever forget the blessings and benefits of being a citizen of Judah. He says that his song would be forever silenced—he would not skillfully play ("my right hand") nor spontaneously sing ("my tongue")—should he forget the marvelous benefits of home.

I believe the sixth verse could trouble some readers. He mentions exalting Jerusalem "above my chief joy." His "chief joy," of course, is that which gave him greatest joy. Why would he exalt a city above his greatest joy? We love our America, but certainly not necessarily more than any earthly joy. It would be strange to exalt America above our highest joy.

The answer is to be found in what the city of Jerusalem *represented* to the writer of this song. It was the place that contained the temple, the place of God's presence, and the center of worship. To be separated from Jerusalem was tantamount to being separated from God and the things of God. You see, in the Old Testament the things of God were spiritually connected to a *place*, Jerusalem. However, in the New Testament the things of God became spiritually connected to a *Person*, the Lord Jesus Christ. That is still true today. We worship a Person—not a building or a location.

The composer is saying that above and beyond his highest joy on earth is Jerusalem and all it represents.

Finally:

Remember, O Lord, against the sons of Edom
The day of Jerusalem,
Who said, "Raze it, raze it,
To its very foundation."
O daughter of Babylon, you devastated one,
How blessed will be the one who repays you
With the recompense with which you have repaid us.
How blessed will be the one who seizes and dashes your little ones
Against the rock. [vv. 7–9]

It doesn't take a Bible scholar to discover that these are exceedingly emotional words. The writer feels passionate regarding the enemies of his beloved Zion. He mentions the ancient enemy of Edom in verse 7, then Babylon in verse 8. While brimming with zeal, he pronounces blessings upon those God may use to avenge the enemies for their brutal and unmerciful treatment of the Jews. The critic reads this (especially verse 9) and attacks the Old Testament for its outrageous God of wrath. If you and I were of that vintage, it is doubtful that the lyrics of Psalm 137 would seem barbaric.

You probably recall the Adolph Eichman trial of the past. One of our national periodicals covered the account in vivid detail. The journalist mentioned a Jewish man who had lost his parents and other close relatives in the horrible Nazi concentration camps. He stood abruptly to his feet in the audience of that courtroom and cursed Eichman. He was told to sit down and restrain himself, which he refused to do. As he was escorted by force from the room, he screamed words to this effect: "Let me get my hands on that Nazi pig . . . just for sixty seconds . . . let me have him that I may torture him with my own hands!" No one criticized that man who screamed those violent words. In fact, the magazine reporter expressed sympathy. Why? Because the man had suffered such a terrible loss, his memory was full and running over with rage. He longed for retribution.

Note that the psalmist doesn't ask that *he* himself might bring vengeance . . . only that God might see that in the end vengeance be poured out in the same way it had been brought upon Judah. If you will pause and read Isaiah 13:14–16, you will see that the Babylonians brutally murdered the little Jewish children before their parents' eyes. With passionate pleas, the writer of this song concludes with a request for similar retribution. He rests his case with God.

Did God respond? Did the Lord ever deal with Babylon and make it "an everlasting desolation" as He promised in Jeremiah 25:12? Yes, indeed! The Persians moved in upon the Babylonians and literally wiped Babylon off the face of the earth, so that it remains a desolation to this day.

Most any world atlas that bothers to mention Babylon will do so with an entry that reads something like: "Babylon, ruins of. . . ." Babylon is still a desolate, barren land of silence along the Bagdad railway, little more than a wind-whipped whistle stop for archaeologists en route to a dig in the rugged wasteland.

Psalm 137 is certainly relevant. It speaks to the believer who suffers the consequence of his sin . . . who tries in vain to "sing the Lord's song in a foreign land." It turns our hearts to Him alone, who can satisfy our deepest needs. It gives us a pattern to follow when we have been severely treated . . . and it reminds us that our God is fully able to bring vengeance upon those who revile and persecute and say all manner of evil against us falsely. As Romans 12:19–21 reminds us, God can and will handle our every desire for retribution, and He can do it in such a thorough way, we need only to step aside and let Him work.

If you are enduring the grind of lingering consequences following a time of disobedience in your life, you understand this song. As you read it, remember that you are not alone in your agonizing heartache. The pain may be severe and lingering, but the good news is this: It is *not* endless.

 EFLECTIONS ON
LINGERING
CONSEQUENCES

1. Think of a few consequences from your past that you were forced to endure. Pause right now and thank the Lord for His grace. Instead of removing you from the earth, He sustained you. He, to this day, allows you to live. Call to mind the magnificence of His wondrous grace. Sing a few bars of "Amazing Grace" and listen again to the lyrics of that grand old hymn.

2. Let's make Psalm 137 a relevant, prophetic warning, not just a matter of historical record. The next time you are tempted to yield and let your carnal nature be satisfied, read the first five verses of this song. It would be a good idea to type those verses on a three-by-five card and clip it to the visor on your car or slide it beneath the glass on your desk. Underline the fourth verse in red.

3. Throughout the balance of this week, pray for any Christian you can think of who has fallen . . . a husband or wife, a politician, a minister, a career person, a physician, a nurse, an attorney, an author, a counselor, a musician, an artist, a camp director, a secretary—anyone! Ask God to bring each one back to Himself. Pray for wisdom and for discernment to know how to respond. Think of possible ways *you* might be able to help set the "captive" free.

PSALM

For the choir director.
A Psalm of David.

O Lord, Thou hast searched me
and known me.
Thou dost know when I sit
down and when I rise up;
Thou dost understand my thought from
afar.
Thou dost scrutinize my path and my
lying down,
And art intimately acquainted with all
my ways.
Even before there is a word on my
tongue,
Behold, O Lord, Thou dost know it all.
Thou hast enclosed me behind and
before,
And laid Thy hand upon me.
Such knowledge is too wonderful for me;
It is too high, I cannot attain to it.

Where can I go from Thy spirit?
Or where can I flee from Thy presence?
If I ascend to heaven, Thou art there;
If I make my bed in Sheol, behold, Thou
art there.
If I take the wings of the dawn,
If I dwell in the remotest part of the sea,
Even there Thy hand will lead me,
And Thy right hand will lay hold of me.
If I say, "Surely the darkness will
overwhelm me,
And the light around me will be night,"
Even the darkness is not dark to Thee,
And the night is as bright as the day.
Darkness and light are alike to
Thee.   [139:1–12]

THE GRIND OF
INSIGNIFICANCE

Most folks struggle with feelings of insignificance from time to time. Larger-than-life athletes, greatly gifted film and television stars, brilliant students, accomplished singers, skillful writers, even capable ministers can leave us feeling intimidated, overlooked, and underqualified. For some, feeling insignificant is not simply a periodic battle; it is a daily grind! We know deep down inside we're valuable; but when we compare ourselves, we often come out on the short end. A well-kept secret is that many of those athletes, celebrities, authors, and preachers who seem so confident struggle with the very same feelings that plague their admirers.

Because of our rapid population explosion, we are becoming numbers and statistical units rather than meaningful individuals. Machines are slowly taking the place of workers. Computers can do much more, much faster, and with greater accuracy than even skilled specialists. Science doesn't help the problem. Our universe is viewed by scientists as being vast, so vast that this Earth is insignificant—a speck of matter surrounded by galaxies measured by light years rather than miles. The immensity of it all overwhelms an earthling at times and forces us to ask the age-old questions: Who am I? Why am I here? Where do I fit? What does it matter? This can result in an inner tailspin—one that increases rather than lessens, as we get older and the awareness of our surroundings expands. Perhaps you are among the many who are passing through what is called an "identity crisis."

If you are wrestling with this very real and puzzling perplex-·
ity, here is a song that is tailor-made for you. It is one of David's
best! His lyrics describe the person who is standing alone and
searching for answers regarding himself, his world, and his
God. It provides the reader with a calm certainty that there is a
definite link between himself and his Lord—that no one has
been flung haphazardly or accidentally into time and space.
This ancient song makes God seem real, personal, and involved
because, in fact, *He is.* The crucial problems of international af-
fairs and "global saturation" suddenly appear not half as crucial
and the difficulties connected with one's identity crisis begin to
fade as this wonderful song is understood.

Psalm 139 answers four questions. As we read through all
twenty-four verses, we find that it falls neatly into four sections
. . . six verses each. Each section deals with a different question. An outline might look something like this:

   I. How well does God know me? (vv. 1–6)
  II. How close is God to me? (vv. 7–12)
 III. How carefully has God made me? (vv. 13–18)
 IV. How much does God protect/help me? (vv. 19–24)

All twenty-four verses link us, God's creation, with our Creator. We are super-important to our Maker. We are not unimpor-
tant specks in space or insignificant nobodies on Earth, but
rather the objects of His care and close, personal attention. If
you take your time and think about each section, you'll find that
the four questions deal with four of our most human and basic
problems:

How well does God know me?
  (*The problem of identity*)

How close is God to me?
  (*The problem of loneliness*)

How carefully has God made me?
  (*The problem of self-image*)

How much will God protect/help me?
(*The problem of fear/worry*)

One final thought before we embark on an analysis of the first twelve verses (we'll examine the final twelve next week): All the way through these verses we read of "the Lord," "His Spirit," "God" . . . and "me," "I," "my." To the psalmist, God is there; better than that, *God is here*. He is reachable, knowable, available, and real. All alienation is removed. All strained formalities and religious protocol are erased. Not only is He *here*, but He is *involved* and *interested* in each individual on this speck-of-a-planet called Earth.

Let's start with the first question.

HOW WELL DOES GOD KNOW ME?

In the first *four* verses of David's song, we are given sufficient information to discover that *God is omniscient* . . . He knows everything. Read the following lyrics slowly and aloud:

> O Lord, Thou hast searched me and known me.
> Thou does know when I sit down and when I rise up;
> Thou dost understand my thought from afar.
> Thou dost scrutinize my path and my lying down,
> And art intimately acquainted with all my ways.
> Even before there is a word on my tongue,
> Behold, O Lord, Thou does know it all. [vv. 1–4]

The songwriter says that God *searches* him. The Hebrew term that led to this translation originally meant "to explore" and sometimes conveyed the idea of digging into or digging through something. To put it in popular terms, "O Lord—you *dig* me!" The thought is that God explores, digs into, and examines me through and through. In the next sentence David pictures himself in two phases of life—passive (sitting down) and active (rising up). Our most common and casual moments are completely familiar to our Lord. Furthermore, even our *thoughts* are an open book. Thoughts come into our minds through a series of distant, fleeting conceptions as microscopic nerves relate to one another in the brain through a complicated process of connections. Even *those* are known by our Lord. That is what David means by God's understanding "my thought from afar." Plutarch, the first-century Greek biographer, had this in mind when he wrote:

> Man may not see thee do an impious deed;
> But God thy very inmost thoughts can read.

We can see thoughts enter people's heads as their faces "light up" or, in some other way telegraph the entrance of ideas. We can hear thoughts as they leave people's minds through their mouths. But we cannot see what happens *between* the entrance and the exit. God can. In fact, God understands what prompts us to think certain thoughts. He therefore understands the hidden, unspoken motives behind our actions.

One Christmas we bought our small children an "Ant City." It was a plastic ant bed filled with a narrow sheet of sand, built out of transparent material that allowed you to watch the inner workings of the insects. Normally, all you can see in an ant bed in the ground are these busy little creatures crawling in and out of their hole. But this interesting "Ant City" allowed us to watch what happened after the ants went into their holes—we could watch these small insects as they journeyed through their tunnels. That is exactly what verse 2 is saying about our thought-life before God. He monitors the entire process.

I appreciate the *New American Standard Bible's* rendering of the third verse: "Thou dost scrutinize my path. . . ." The verb *scrutinize* is a translation of the Hebrew word which means "to sift." It is the idea of submitting oneself to minute scrutiny. God carefully sifts away at our choices and decisions. As a result of this phenomenal insight, He is thoroughly acquainted with us—and I mean thoroughly! To put the finishing touches on the facts of God's omniscience, He knows our words even *before* we utter them, which causes David to write: "Thou does know it all. . . ." God knows every word of every language in every human being on every continent at every moment of every day. Think of it!

Matthew 10:30 adds the capstone: ". . . the very hairs of your head are all numbered." It is not that God concerns Himself with mental and verbal trivia; it is simply that He is omniscient, that He is fully and accurately aware of everything at all times, the visible as well as the invisible, the public as well as the private.

One articulate theologian explains God's omniscience like this:

> To say that God is omniscient is to say that He possesses perfect knowledge and therefore has no need to learn. But it is more: it is to say that God has never learned and cannot learn. . . . God perfectly knows Himself and, being the source and author of all things, it follows that He knows all that can be known. And this He knows instantly and with a fullness of perfection that includes every possible item of knowledge concerning everything that exists or could have existed anywhere in the universe at any time in the past or that may exist in the centuries or ages yet unborn. . . . Because God knows all things perfectly, He knows no thing better than any other thing, but all things equally well . . . He is never surprised, never amazed, He never wonders about anything nor . . . does He seek information . . . our heavenly Father knows us completely. No talebearer can inform on us, no enemy can make an accusation stick; no forgotten skeleton can come tumbling out of some hidden closet to abash us and expose our past; no unsuspected weakness in our characters can come to light to turn God away from us, since He knew us utterly before we knew Him and called us to Himself in the full knowledge of everything that was against us.[15]

How well does God know you? These first four verses enable you to realize that He could not possibly know you better! Just in case the grind of insignificance is still doing a number on you, ponder the fact that you are the object of the living God's attention every moment of every day of your life!

Now consider the next two verses of Psalm 139:

> Thou hast enclosed me behind and before,
> And laid Thy hand upon me.
> Such knowledge is too wonderful for me;
> It is too high, I cannot attain to it. [vv. 5–6]

David now mentions *God's omnipotence;* He is in full control, He is all-powerful. Knowing us as He does, He puts the necessary controls upon us. The fact that He "encloses" us could be misunderstood. This is the translation of a Hebrew term used for the besieging of a city in battle—closing off all escape routes. One Hebrew scholar says it means "to be hemmed in." The idea is that God has us in inescapable situations and there steadies us, directs us, restrains us, keeps us from running and escaping from that situation. This explains why His hand is upon us.

Perhaps the apostle Paul was in such a predicament when he said he and his companions were "burdened excessively, beyond our strength" (2 Cor. 1:8). The King James Version renders those words: "we were pressed out of measure, above strength." The Greek term means "to be weighed down." It's the idea of intense *pressure:* "we were under tremendous pressure." In pressurized situations today God shuts off all escape routes, but He stays *Isa. 43* *(esp. v. 2)* near and steadies us with His hand so that you and I might learn valuable lessons instead of running from the pressure. Annie Johnson Flint describes scenes familiar to all of us—times of inescapable pressure:

> Pressed out of measure and pressed to all length;
> Pressed so intensely it seems beyond strength.
> Pressed in the body and pressed in the soul;
> Pressed in the mind till the dark surges roll;
> Pressure by foes, and pressure by friends;
> Pressure on pressure, till life nearly ends.
> Pressed into loving the staff and the rod;
> Pressed into knowing no helper but God.
> Pressed into liberty where nothing clings;
> Pressed into faith for impossible things.
> Pressed into living a life in the Lord;
> Pressed into living a Christ-life outpoured.[16]

After contemplating all these truths, David exclaims, in effect, "It blows my mind!" (v. 6). So wonderful were these proofs of God's knowledge and control, he could not begin to contain his emotions. His *problem of identity* has begun to fade as the songwriter realizes God views His creatures as important and significant. He knows us. He scrutinizes our lives. He studies us and steadies us twenty-four hours a day. Although it blows our minds to comprehend it, it is true. How well does God know me? TOTALLY!

A related question follows on the heels of that first one.

HOW CLOSE IS GOD TO ME?

All right, so God knows me and controls me; so what? He can do that at a distance, through millions and millions of light years of space. What I want to know is this: *Is He near?* Perhaps that is your reaction to the first few verses of Psalm 139. What you'd like to know has to do with closeness. Is He really up close and in touch? Yes, God is near. He is no distant, preoccupied Deity. In fact, *He is omnipresent.* In verse 7, David states this in the form of two questions: "Where can I go from Thy Spirit? / Or where can I flee from Thy presence?"

The rebellious prophet Jonah must have wondered: "Can I find any place that will remove me from God?" He found out the hard way that the answer is an emphatic "No!" David puts it in terms anyone can understand.

> If I ascend to heaven, Thou art there;
> If I make my bed in Sheol, behold, Thou art there.
> If I take the wings of the dawn,
> If I dwell in the remotest part of the sea,
> Even there Thy hand will lead me,
> And Thy right hand will lay hold of me. [Ps. 139:8–10]

In the Hebrew Bible, the pronouns referring to God are abrupt and emphatic: "If I go up to heaven—THOU! If I go down to the grave—THOU!"

The next verse carries us out into the vast ocean on "the wings of the dawn." It's a beautiful expression, but what does it mean? Most likely it describes the rays of the morning sun that flash across the sky. Perhaps we could paraphrase it more technically by saying: "If I could travel the speed of light. . . ." Just think of that! By traveling at such speed, I would get to the moon in less than two seconds—Thou! (God would meet me.) It would take about four years to reach the first star at that speed, and again—Thou! (God would be there as well.) Omnipresence simply means there is no place He is *not.*

And the huge body of water we call an ocean may make me seem insignificant and remote—but still He is there. He never leaves me lonely—"even there Thy hand will lead me."

The first time I grasped the magnitude of these verses I was in the Marine Corps on a troop ship crossing the Pacific Ocean, bound for the Orient. It took seventeen days. The ocean swells on stormy days were forty to fifty feet high; and when our ship was down in the bowels of the swell, the crest loomed above like a giant domed building about to fall on us. As we would rise up to the peak, we could see nothing but water all around— deep, blue-black swells, never-ending across the horizon, 360 degrees around. I remember opening my Bible early one morning to Psalm 139:7–10 and, honestly, I almost shouted. Talk about an object lesson—I *was* one! I suddenly felt at ease in His presence. My loneliness seemed utterly foolish. His hand was leading me, His right hand was holding me right there in the "remotest part of the sea." Though I was literally insignificant by comparison, a calm, secure feeling swept over me.

That is the point David is communicating here. God is never absent.

And now in verses 11 and 12, he announces that not even darkness affects God's pervading presence:

> If I say, "Surely the darkness will overwhelm me,
> And the light around me will be night,"
> Even the darkness is not dark to Thee,
> And the night is as bright as the day.
> Darkness and light are alike to Thee.

There were times in my childhood when I would occasionally feel fearful at night. (You may recall having similar feelings.) At those times I would grab the covers and snatch them over my head. I can still remember tucking myself far down beneath them, thinking that I would be kept from harm. How childish . . . and yet, how much like adults!

Somehow, we may think, *If I do this in the darkness, it will go unnoticed.* This ancient song reminds us that it won't! Even the darkness is not dark to the Lord. According to Hebrews 4:13, there is not a creature hidden from Him. We need never feel lonely. He sees it all . . . and best of all, He cares.

That's enough for this week. We'll conclude this song next week. It has been rich to glean encouragement from the composer's thoughts, hasn't it? God cares for you and me. How very much He cares! He does so because we are important to Him. The grind of feeling insignificant is diminished as the truth of David's song emerges.

EFLECTIONS ON INSIGNIFICANCE

1. Tonight, step outside. If the air is clear and the sky cloudless, look up. Why not go ahead, lie down flat on your back, and stare at those incredible stars? Stay long enough to allow your mind to grasp the immensity of the galaxy above you. It is easy to forget that what you are observing may seem vast, but it is only one galaxy among many! Remind yourself that you are more significant to your God than any one *or all* of those planets and stars in the stellar spaces. After all, they are ultimately going to pass away, but you are eternal. Give Him your grateful thanks.

2. In the early part of Psalm 139, David mentioned God's knowing your actions, your location, your words, your thoughts, and your entire situation. He then exploded with one of his "It's too much, Lord!" exclamations. What seems "too much" to you? Which part of the song makes you shake your head in amazement? Have you told Him . . . or anyone else? Do so.

3. Many people I know are still a little fearful of the dark. Look back at verses 11–12. It's possible you, too, feel uneasy after nightfall. Commit both of these verses to memory. Start saying them to yourself whenever you step into the darkness. See if just the reminder of His presence in the darkness doesn't help relieve some of your fears.

*P*SALM

For the choir director.
A Psalm of David.

For Thou didst form my inward
     parts;
Thou didst weave me in my
     mother's womb.
I will give thanks to Thee, for I am
     fearfully and wonderfully made;
Wonderful are Thy works,
And my soul knows it very well.
My frame was not hidden from Thee,
When I was made in secret,
And skillfully wrought in the depths of
     the earth.
Thine eyes have seen my unformed
     substance;
And in Thy book they were all written,
The days that were ordained for me,
When as yet there was not one of them.

How precious also are Thy thoughts to
     me, O God!
How vast is the sum of them!

If I should count them, they would
    outnumber the sand.
When I awake, I am still with Thee.

O that Thou wouldst slay the wicked, O
    God;
Depart from me, therefore, men of
    bloodshed.
For they speak against Thee wickedly,
And Thine enemies take Thy name in
    vain.
Do I not hate those who hate Thee, O
    Lord?
And do I not loathe those who rise up
    against Thee?
I hate them with the utmost hatred;
They have become my enemies.

Search me, O God, and know my heart;
Try me and know my anxious thoughts;
And see if there be any hurtful way in
    me,
And lead me in the everlasting
    way.   [139:13–24]

THE GRIND OF INSECURITY

Let's begin this week with a few words of review. Psalm 139 links us with God. It, like few other scriptures, connects us with our Creator. You'll recall it answers four of the most frequently asked questions that come to our minds about God:

> How well does God know me? (vv. 1– 6)
> How close is God to me? (vv. 7–12)
> How carefully has God made me? (vv. 13–18)
> How much will God protect/help me? (vv. 19–24)

Haven't you asked yourself such things before? Sure you have! Everyone has. Built into all of us is a curiosity that longs to be satisfied, especially regarding the One who created this world.

Last week we looked at the first twelve verses of this great song. From the first six verses we discovered that God *knows* us thoroughly and completely. We found that He knows our private, quiet moments just as well as He knows our public and active times. We learned that He not only knows our thoughts and our words, but He even knows them before they are lodged in our brains or expressed from our mouths . . . God knows everything about everyone, every moment of every day—God is *omniscient*. Furthermore, we learned that God is in full control. Nothing occurs outside the realm of His sovereign will—God is *omnipotent*.

In the next six verses we found that He who knows us is always *near* us. No place we may travel, regardless of the speed of our vehicle, causes us to be lost from His sight or distant from Him. Not even darkness separates us from Him. How amazing! Darkness is just like light to God. Nothing could begin to separate Him from us or, for that matter, make Him nearer to us. Both are impossible. God is *omnipresent*.

HOW CAREFULLY HAS GOD MADE ME?

"Okay," you reply. "The song makes beautiful poetry and declares great theology, but how can I be sure it is all true?" A subtle uncertainty grinds away in most of us. One of the best proofs that God is and does all these things is *the design of your body*. Consider how carefully He has made you. Verses 13–16 address this. In my opinion this section of biblical truth is one of the most remarkable revelations in all of Scripture. Remember, it was written by David in a day when anatomy and embryology were relatively unknown subjects—at best, primitive. Yet here in this ancient song the prenatal stages of development are set forth with phenomenal simplicity and insight. The point David declares is this: Only a God who knows us and is near us could be so intimately involved in making us.

Verse 12 tells us of darkness and the inability of humanity to hide from God. Previous verses speak of hidden or remote places as being well-known and under the perpetual surveillance of God. Verse 13 goes even further. It transports us into *the womb*, a place of intimacy and darkness. It is here that the songwriter builds his case.

Verse 13

> For Thou didst form my inward parts;
> Thou didst weave me in my mother's womb.

The *Thou* is highly emphatic. The idea is "You, Yourself, and no other. . . ." It is neither "nature" nor "Mother Nature" who forms the miracle in the womb; it is God alone . . . and no other. Linger over the term *form*. When this verb appears in the original Hebrew, it often carries the idea of "originate." God originates our inward parts. It may surprise you to know that those two words—*inward parts*—literally mean "kidneys." In ancient times the kidneys were symbolic of all our vital organs—kidney, heart, lung, liver, etc. In fact, the verse goes on to say that God did "weave me together" in the womb. The verb *sah-nack* suggests the idea of knitting together like an interwoven mass or thicket. God is involved in placing all the organs and various parts of our body together into such a well-knitted fashion, it forms a veritable "thicket" of muscle, tendons, bone, blood, veins, and arteries.

Let me paraphrase verse 13 in order to bring out some of the color in the original text:

> For God alone—none other—originated my vital organs (such as my kidneys). You knitted my inner being together in the womb of my mother.

Verse 14

Verse 14 causes the writer to burst forth in praise. Observe his spontaneous words of grateful amazement:

> I will give thanks to Thee, for I am fearfully and wonderfully made;
> Wonderful are Thy works,
> And my soul knows it very well.

Isn't this true? We are a species of wonder. No one would argue that the human body is a phenomenal combination of strength, beauty, coordination, grace, and balance on the outside. But if you think the outside is remarkable, just glance *inside*. Talk about something wonderful!

Verse 15

Verse 15 describes our origin:

> My frame was not hidden from Thee,
> When I was made in secret,
> And skillfully wrought in the depths of the earth.

We sometimes refer to our bodily shape as our "frame." The original Hebrew term here means "bony substance" or "skeleton." Our skeletons were not hidden from God when they were made "in secret . . . in the depths of the earth." This is an idiomatic expression for a protected place, a concealed and safe place—as one may hide his treasure by burying it. No doubt this "secret place" is a reference to the womb. The Hebrew word translated *skillfully wrought* literally means "variegated" . . . like a multicolored piece of cloth. Moses used the same Hebrew term in Exodus when he referred to the making of the curtains in the ancient tabernacle. The idea is similar to an embroidered piece of tapestry or a work of fine needlepoint. The picture must include the concept of our veins and arteries, "embroidered" like variegated threads within the body. God is *that* involved in the making of our bodies. He is like a careful, skillful artist who takes great pain with each color and stroke.

Again, a paraphrase:

> My skeleton and bones were not hidden from You when I was made in that concealed place of protection, when my veins and arteries were skillfully embroidered together in variegated colors like fine needlepoint.

The truth of all this was brought home to me several years ago in a conversation I had with a young man doing his medical internship. He was studying to be a surgeon. He commented on the beautiful "color scheme" God has placed within our inner bodies. He stated that there are definite colors in our various organs . . . that the veins and arteries almost make the inner network appear "variegated" in color. He smiled when I informed him that that is exactly what David wrote in his song centuries ago.

Verse 16

This verse adds the capstone:

> Thine eyes have seen my unformed substance;
> And in Thy book they were all written,
> The days that were ordained for me,
> When as yet there was not one of them.

God's eyes were fixed upon my "unformed substance," says David. The Hebrew verb from which this descriptive statement is taken means "to fold together, to wrap up." In its noun form it appears only here in the Old Testament, and it means "embryo." In other words, David is saying: "In my very first hours and days of life after conception—when I was still wrapped up in embryonic form—God was watching over me. He was never absent nor unconcerned." Frankly, it is impossible to read these verses and deny that an unborn fetus is a living human being. From the very earliest moments after conception, God is at work in the mother's womb. Talk about a case against abortion!

The verse goes on to address life *after* birth. Not only does God concern Himself with us between conception and birth, but He also sets His attention upon us between birth and death. Look closely at this sixteenth verse. Looking at life from God's vantage point, David says that our heavenly Father marks out our days and "ordains" them even before we are born ". . . When as yet there was not one of them." The original term translated *ordain* is often used in the Old Testament in connection with a potter who forms clay on his wheel, shaping and pressing and pulling at it until it takes the shape he has in mind. God forms our days so that they are exactly the kind of days we should have to become the kind of person He wants us to be. There is little room left for insecurity once we understand His constant interest in our lives.

Verses 17–18

David is again on the crest of ecstasy as he exclaims:

> How precious also are Thy thoughts to me, O God!
> How vast is the sum of them!
> If I should count them, they would outnumber the sand.
> When I awake, I am still with Thee.

In today's terms this great songwriter might say: "How valuable! How mighty and vast! Your thoughts and your plans for me are magnificent, O God! You carefully and meticulously form me in the womb, you arrange and appoint my days so that each twenty-four-hour period does its part in shaping me into Your kind of person . . . and (grace heaped upon grace!) when death invades, I awake in Your presence—still with Thee."

Let me put these inspired lyrics together so that the paraphrase includes much of what we have discovered:

> For You, God, and none other, originated my vital organs (such as my kidneys). You knitted me together in the womb of my mother. . . . My skeleton and bones were not hidden from You when I was made in that concealed place of protection, when my veins and arteries were skillfully embroidered together in variegated colors like fine needlepoint. Your eyes watched over me when I was just an embryo; and in Your book the days I should experience were all described and recorded—the kind of days that would shape me into the person You want me to be—even before I had been born. How priceless and mighty and vast and numerous are Your thoughts of me, O God! Should I attempt to count them, they would outnumber the sand on the seashore. And Your plan isn't limited just to *this* life. Should I die, I would awaken securely in Your arms—I would be with You more than ever before.

HOW MUCH WILL GOD PROTECT/HELP ME?

The grind of insecurity begins to slow down when we grasp how perfectly God designed each one of us, and especially when we cap it off with how much He helps us.

Verses 19–22

The songwriter doesn't mince his words in these verses:

> O that Thou wouldst slay the wicked, O God;
> Depart from me, therefore, men of bloodshed.
> For they speak against Thee wickedly,
> And Thine enemies take Thy name in vain.
> Do I not hate those who hate Thee, O Lord?
> And do I not loathe those who rise up against Thee?
> I hate them with the utmost hatred;
> They have become my enemies. [Ps. 139:19–22]

The subject on his heart is clearly expressed:

The wicked (v. 19a)
Men of bloodshed (v. 19b)
Thine enemies (v. 20)
Those who hate/rise up against Thee (v. 21)
My enemies (v. 22)

On six separate occasions David refers to the enemies of God in the strongest of terms. These were not moderate, passive foes of the Lord; they were unashamed, hateful, open, and blatant despisers of God and God's people. To associate with them would pollute the testimony of any saint—and David declares his independence of them, especially when he says, ". . . They have become my enemies" (v. 22b).

Exactly what does David ask of God? One specific thing is requested: "Slay the wicked!" (v. 19a). To him, the God of heaven is marvelous, pure, holy, just, and good. His desire was to be the same—just as we are told to be in Ephesians 5:1, which says: "Therefore be imitators of God, as beloved children."

David wanted to imitate God. He longed to be a godly man—perhaps more than any other king in the history of Israel, which may explain why he was called "a man after God's own heart." He wanted to be removed from every enemy of God, lest he become swayed and stained by their wickedness. This shouldn't be taken as a bloodthirsty, brutal plea . . . nor a self-righteous, super-spiritual prayer. He was supremely interested in being God's man, regardless. In his zeal for righteousness, he asked God's help in protecting him from those who stood against the things he held dear. To David, a man of war, the only solution for God was to "slay the wicked!" He did not hesitate to request that of Him.

Before I move on, let me ask you: With whom do you spend most of your time? How close are you to those who defy and deny the name of your Savior? How deep a friendship have you nurtured with people who are out-and-out enemies of right-eousness? Could the answers to those questions explain your battle with insecurity?

Charles Spurgeon once wrote: "Godless men are not the stuff out of which true friends can ever be made."[17] True words! While I am not encouraging our isolating ourselves from all lost people, I *am* saying that a close companionship with haters of God will take a damaging toll on our spiritual life. The virus of the degen-erate heart is dangerously contagious, and you cannot spend much time near those who have it without eventually suffering from the same disease. This is as true for the teenager who wants "popularity at any cost" as it is for the businessman who prostitutes his convictions for an extra buck. Spiritual compro-mise is a deadly problem! We have already looked at 1 Corinthi-ans 15:33 on more than one occasion since we began our year-long scriptural safari, but it's worth repeating here: "Do not be deceived: 'Bad company corrupts good morals.'"

Verse 20

In Psalm 139:20, David lists two characteristics that identify God's enemies:

1. They speak against God (they are irreverent).
2. They take His name in vain (they use profanity).

Isn't it interesting that wicked people reveal their wickedness through their tongue? Irreverence and profanity are the trademarks of deep heart problems. Mark it down: a foul, irreverent tongue is the byproduct of a foul, irreverent heart.

Because David trusted God to protect him by slaying his enemies, he did not try to take matters into his own hands . . . nor did he attempt to clean up the lives of God's enemies. Both would be futile efforts. He left the final decision with his Lord—a very wise and biblical action to take, by the way.

Verse 23-24

Before David closes hymn 139, he makes a final request of God in verses 23–24. The words are familiar to many Christians.

> Search me, O God, and know my heart;
> Try me and know my anxious thoughts;
> And see if there be any hurtful way in me,
> And lead me in the everlasting way.

David no longer looks *up* (as in verses 1–18) nor *around* (as in verses 19–22); he now looks *within*. He wants to be God's man at any cost, so he invites the Lord to make a thorough examination of him down deep inside. The word *search* was used earlier in verse 1. The basic idea of the original Hebrew verb, you may remember, means "to explore, dig, probe." David wants God to penetrate his outer shell and dig down deeply within him. He unveils his inner being, down where unspoken thoughts dwell and unstated motives hide out in secret, and he invites God's searchlight.

Now David goes even further. He asks the Lord to put him to the test so as to discover any distracting thoughts. In other words, he is saying, "Find out which thoughts carry me away from fellowship with You, O God. Show them to me so that I can understand them and their effect on my walk with You." That was his desire. Insecurity has passed off the scene as he stands open before his Lord.

The desired result of this probing is set forth in the last verse, where David asks God to see if there is any way of pain or grief in him. It is not that *God* might know the results, but that he himself—David—might know what God discovered. When you submit yourself to the scalpel of the surgeon for an exploratory operation, you do it *not* just for the sake of the physician. *You* want to know the findings yourself, don't you? You are interested in what is discovered. David finally states that it is his desire to be led "in the everlasting way" . . . meaning the path of righteousness. I repeat, he wanted to be a man of God, regardless.

Do *you* want to be a person whose walk with God is intimate and deep? Honestly now, is Christianity simply a ticket to heaven for you, or is it the very root and foundation of your life? Is this business of Bible reading/study, prayer, church attendance, baptism, witnessing, the Lord's Table, and the singing of hymns just something to calm your guilt and/or occupy your Sundays? On the other hand, if Christ has gotten a solid grasp of your will and you've become genuinely serious about spiritual things, then you will take the truth of these verses and allow it to take root in your life. Becoming a godly person takes time, but along the way it includes occasions when you expose your entire inner being to God's searching and you welcome any insight He might give you, regardless of the difficulty involved in facing it. By and by, the daily grind of insecurity will fade and you will be saying to the Lord: "I gladly open all the closets of my life . . . every room and every corner. Scrutinize my thoughts and examine my motives, Lord. Show me what needs attention. Reveal to me what brings pain to You in my life."

 EFLECTIONS ON INSECURITY

1. What a rich, revealing song David composed! As you look back over that center section of Psalm 139 (verses 13–18), what helps you the most?

   • The thought that He was watching over you from the time of conception?

   • The way He wove your organs and muscles and personality together?

   • The fact that He determined your appearance and structure and height before birth?

   Why? What caused you to choose the one you did?

2. Think about the implications of the verses we just considered. Why are they so damaging to those who say there is no problem with having an abortion . . . "after all there isn't really a life until birth" we are told. Use verses 13–16 to refute that position.

3. The final "benediction" of the song (verses 23–24) is quite a vulnerable prayer. Have you prayed it this week? If not, do so now. Utter the words aloud. As God "searches" and "tries" you . . . pay attention. If He reveals a "hurtful way" to you, be ready to deal with it.

Maskil of David, when he was in the cave.
A Prayer.

I cry aloud with my voice to the Lord;
I make supplication with my voice to
the Lord.
I pour out my complaint before Him;
I declare my trouble before Him.
When my spirit was overwhelmed within
me,
Thou didst know my path.
In the way where I walk
They have hidden a trap for me.
Look to the right and see;
For there is no one who regards me;
There is no escape for me;
No one cares for my soul.

I cried out to Thee, O Lord;
I said, "Thou art my refuge,
My portion in the land of the living.
Give heed to my cry,
For I am brought very low;
Deliver me from my persecutors,
For they are too strong for me.
Bring my soul out of prison,
So that I may give thanks to Thy name;
The righteous will surround me.
For Thou wilt deal bountifully with
me." [142:1–7]

THE GRIND OF DEPRESSION

Who hasn't struggled with those demoralizing seasons of dark depression? Some get so low and stay there so long they decide that taking their lives is better than enduring it any longer. Others seem to go in and out . . . down, then back up again. Depression has been described as a black hole, an abysmal cave. It certainly includes discouraging feelings that refuse to go away. I know some who have fought the battle of depression for years! In Book I we addressed the grind of despondency. Depression is much deeper, more complicated, and usually lasts longer. Despondency leaves us feeling listless, blue, and discouraged, but depression is a feeling of severe oppresiveness that is far more serious. If it doesn't lift, professional help is often necessary, though not always. Mysteriously, there are occasions when hope returns rather suddenly and the light begins to shine again. Few joys are greater than that one!

My hope is that this song from David's pen will help bring some long-awaited light into your cave of depression. Before we begin to dig into the first verse of his great hymn, we come across some helpful information in the superscription: *"Maskil of David, when he was in the cave. A Prayer."*

THE OPENING STATEMENT

There are four important parts to this opening statement:
1. "Maskil." Thirteen of the songs in the Hebrews' hymnal

are so designated. As we learned in the previous volume, this is from the Hebrew root verb *sah-kaal,* meaning "to be prudent, wise, to give insight and instruction." It is an *instructive* psalm. It is designed to give us help and insight in a certain area of life. It will assist us so that we may know how to handle a particular situation wisely.

Since Psalm 142 deals with a time of depression in the writer's life, it is a *maskil* designed to give us insight into handling times of great, overwhelming distress.

2. ". . . of David." This assures us that David was the composer of the hymn. Although David did not write *all* the psalms, he wrote more in Israel's ancient hymnal than any other person.

3. ". . . when he was in the cave." The phrase regarding "the cave" appears in only one other superscription—Psalm 57. Unfortunately, David does not designate *which* cave. Two possibilities come to mind—either the cave of Engedi (1 Sam. 24) or Adullam (1 Sam. 22). It was probably the latter—for reasons I'll not take the time to develop here.

To appreciate that which gave birth to this song of depression, listen to the first two verses of 1 Samuel 22:

> So David departed from there and escaped to the cave of Adullam; and when his brothers and all his father's household heard of it, they went down there to him. And everyone who was in distress, and everyone who was in debt, and everyone who was discontented, gathered to him; and he became captain over them. Now there were about four hundred men with him.

Talk about adding insult to injury! Here's our friend David, running for his life from madman Saul, finally finding relief and solitude in a dark cave. His relief is short-lived, however, as his solitude is invaded by a solid stream of "everyone who was in distress, and everyone who was in debt, and everyone who was discontented . . . about four hundred men." Just imagine! Four hundred failures. Four hundred malcontents. Four hundred *plus one*—David.

The four hundred were an unorganized, inefficient, depressed mob without a leader, so David was "elected" to be in charge. Picture the scene in your mind. With a little imagination you could see how depressed he must have been. Surely he sighed as he thought, *What now?* or *Why me?* Well, whatever else he did, he also wrote a song—Psalm 142. In the depth of distress and at the end of his rope he talked with his Lord about his desperate situation. So much for the cave.

4. A Prayer. Spurgeon says: "Caves make good closets for prayer."[18] True words. This psalm is actually a prayer, so we should handle it with respect. Prayers were not recorded in Scripture for the purpose of analysis, but to bring insight and encouragement. This psalm is a good one to consider when you find yourself in the same state of mind as David. To put it bluntly, he was back in the pits.

In the first two verses we find David at the mouth of that gloomy cave. The depth of his anguish is clearly expressed. He comes face to face with his God in prayer. (Note: twice he calls "to the Lord" and twice he brings his complaint "before Him.")

> I cry aloud with my voice to the Lord;
> I make supplication with my voice to the Lord.
> I pour out my complaint before Him;
> I declare my trouble before Him.

Verse 1

What is translated in the first verse as "I cry aloud" literally means "I shriek." The original Hebrew term means "to sound as thunder, to bellow." From the interior of that cave, David thunders out his pitiful needs with heartrending groans. "I make supplication" could better be rendered "I implore favor." His self-image had been assaulted. He felt stripped, worthless, and useless—completely depressed. So he asks for evidence of God's favor. He needs to feel needed and necessary. He no longer had honor and respect; self-esteem was, it seemed, forever removed.

When we hit the bottom, we feel this way. Our self-image is shot! In order to be effective, we *must* view ourselves as God views us—favorable, loved, useful, and needed. I have found

that my first step toward a solution is turning "to the Lord"—
going "before Him" as David did. To stay at the bottom, lick my
wounds, and roll in misery leads only to deeper despair. Call
upon Him—*shriek* if you must—but don't sit for days in the
silence of self-pity! God longs to hear your words. Your honest
and forthright declaration is precisely what prayer is all about.
It is a discipline that ignites incredible results.

I used to wonder why we ever needed to utter words in prayer
since God already knows all our thoughts (Ps. 139:4). Then one
day I stumbled across Hosea 14:1–2:

> Return, O Israel, to the Lord your God,
> For you have stumbled because of your iniquity.
> Take words with you and return to the Lord.
> Say to Him, "Take away all iniquity,
> And receive us graciously,
> That we may present the fruit of our lips."

Did you notice the prophet's command? His charge is to "take
words with you. . . ." Saying our most troubling thoughts, expressing our deep-down feelings in words, is a definite therapy.
This way we get those depressive feelings out into the open
. . . we resurrect them from the prisonlike limbo of our inner
being. David did exactly that. He "took words with him" as he
came to terms with his depression.

Verse 2

In the second verse of Psalm 142 the man openly declares his
problem to God: "I pour out my complaint before Him; / I
declare my trouble before Him." Look at that term *trouble*. It
comes from the Hebrew verb meaning "to be bound up, tied
tightly, restricted, narrow, cramped"—or as we would say today, "I'm in a *tight fix*." When he says "I declare my trouble," the
Hebrew word for *declare* literally means "to cause to be conspic-
uous." He wanted *nothing* hidden.

Putting all the preceding thoughts together, the first two
verses could read:

> I shriek with my voice to the Lord;
> I implore favor with my voice to the Lord.
> I pour out, before Him, my complaint;
> My cramped, narrow way, before Him,
> I cause to be conspicuous.

Do you *really* level with God about how you feel and what you are experiencing? Do you get vividly specific? He wants to be your closest Friend, your dearest Counselor. He wants you to keep nothing from Him. Unfortunately, many who suffer lengthy battles with depression do not express what is plaguing them. Some find it almost impossible to articulate thoughts that are brimming with pain or hostility or grief. Most stay to themselves and say very little. David spoke openly of his anguish.

Verse 3

The third verse would speak more literally if we read it:

> When my spirit fainted away within me . . .
> (But You—You Yourself—know my pathway)
> In the way where I walk
> They have concealed a trap for me.

The verse begins with an unfinished sentence. David feels enveloped or wrapped up in his depression, so much so his inner spirit feels faint and feeble. Suddenly, he stops and admits that God knows everything, even his inner feelings. This seems to occur to David rather abruptly. (A parallel passage on this same subject is Job 23:10–17, which you should stop and read. It is magnificent!) David then adds that things on the *outside* of the cave are as depressing as on the *inside*. Traps were laid by Saul and his men. Spies were everywhere. He was a marked man.

Verse 4

Verse 4 rounds out the bleak picture:

> Look to the right and see;
> For there is no one who regards me;

There is no escape for me;
No one cares for my soul.

He invited the Lord to look to his right—the place for a protector and defender to stand—but no one was there. He was alone, humanly speaking. He could not escape. He felt that there was no one who cared for his soul. The poor man is so-o-o-o-o-o depressed!

Perhaps you feel down today, thinking that all hope is gone, that God has abandoned you, that the end has come. Yes, you may feel those things, but that doesn't mean your feelings are true. The Lord of heaven knows the pressure of your feelings. He understands the depths of your distress. Best of all, He is there. He cares. He understands: "The righteous will surround me, / For Thou wilt deal bountifully with me" (142:7).

What faith! David is looking ahead and claiming, by faith, a time of genuine victory. He is declaring that God will again use him and cause others to surround him and look to him for leadership. Why? Because God will deal bountifully with him . . . because God will use these distressing, difficult days to give him maturity and inner strength and stability. Inner healing will come, someday.

Let me repeat what I said earlier in Book I—God doesn't use us in the lives of other people because we *do* some things, but rather because we *are* something. People do not long to be around one who *does* a lot of things as much as they want to be around one who *is* what they admire. It is greatness of character and a life with depth that earns the respect of others. Those who have been honed and buffeted, bruised and melted in the furnace of affliction, and then emerge with emotional stability and inner strength—they are the ones who have a ministry in the lives of others. Their weakness is like a magnet . . . for when we are weak, He is strong.

So then, in summary, if you are in the cave of depression, try your best to look up. Call upon the Lord Jesus Christ. Hold nothing back. You can trust Him to handle whatever you toss in His direction. Tell Him exactly how your situation is affecting you. If you are able, spell out precisely what you need at this time. Rely on Him. Do not doubt and do not waver. Stand firm.

Remember, you are in His schoolroom. He is the Teacher. He is giving you a lengthy examination in the crucible of suffering . . . and no one can give a more complete exam than our Lord!

I commend this song to all who are undergoing the daily grind of depression today. It is food for your soul in the cave as the storm continues to roar.

Hang in there, my friend. He is preparing you for a unique message and an enviable ministry. Believe it or not, that dark cave of depression which seems endless is part of His divine plan. Who knows? The light you have been longing to see could return today.

EFLECTIONS
ON DEPRESSION

1. Describe *your* cave today. Spend a few minutes thinking through the reason you find yourself submerged amidst such dark feelings and dismal outlook. Does it include:
   - something from your recent past?
   - something you feel angry about?
   - something between you and another person?
   - something you resent or thought had ended?
   - something you fear in the future?

   A time of personal analysis can yield a great deal of insight. Take the time to do just that.

2. Do not hesitate to follow David's model. "Cry aloud" with your voice to the Lord. "Pour out" your complaint . . . "declare" your trouble. You can even shriek! Trust me, He can handle *whatever* you serve across the net. He longs to hear you.

3. Have you sought the assistance, the friendship, the counsel of another? Why not start there? Furthermore, have you had a thorough physical exam within the past twelve or eighteen months? If not, do so. People who stay depressed over a long period of time usually become isolated, lonely sufferers. There is a better way. To stay all alone only deepens the cave and intensifies the sadness. Seek help. As I mentioned earlier, it may require some professional assistance. If so, don't hesitate. Caves can be awfully dark and demoralizing. Our minds tend to play tricks on us if we stay in them too long.

P raise the Lord!
Sing to the Lord a new song,
And His praise in the
congregation of the godly
ones.
Let Israel be glad in his Maker;
Let the sons of Zion rejoice in their King.
Let them praise His name with dancing;
Let them sing praises to Him with timbrel
and lyre.
For the Lord takes pleasure in His people;
He will beautify the afflicted ones with
salvation.

Let the godly ones exult in glory;
Let them sing for joy on their beds.
Let the high praises of God be in their
mouth,
And a two-edged sword in their hand,
To execute vengeance on the nations,
And punishment on the peoples;
To bind their kings with chains,
And their nobles with fetters of iron;
To execute on them the judgment written;
This is an honor for all His godly ones.
Praise the Lord!   [149:1–9]

THE GRIND OF PRAISE-LESS TIMES

There are times when the hardest words in the world to utter are *Praise the Lord* (also translated "Hallelujah!"). These words just don't flow from our lips. In fact, there are times we are turned off even when *others* use the words!

In the final five psalms, interestingly, each one begins with that statement of praise. Perhaps by focusing on one of the five, we will uncover some things that will help us live beyond the grind of praise-less times.

If you are a Christian and have spent much time in churches and Christian groups, you have heard "Hallelujah!" dozens, even hundreds, of times. But what does it actually mean? We hear it and we say it without realizing its significance. In the next few pages, I want to explore its meaning with you. These five concluding "Hallelujah Psalms" form the most beautiful scenery on the last leg of our journey through the ancient hymnal—a journey that has often included times of sadness, sin, gloom, loneliness, distress, and depression.

I recall returning to the United States after a lengthy tour of duty on Okinawa and other Oriental islands and countries. As our troop ship sailed under the beautiful Golden Gate Bridge, tears came to my eyes! All the loneliness, sadness, and distress of my previous months away from my homeland and wife and family faded from significance because of that final lap into the harbor of San Francisco. That is the way it is in our study of the songs in Scripture. The beauty and loveliness of the final scene tend to make us forget the many days the composers spent in heartache and sorrow.

Hallelujah is literally a Hebrew term, not English. It is a composite word, made up of two smaller terms—*hah-lale*, meaning "to boast," and *Yah-weh*, meaning "Jehovah." Putting them together, the exact meaning is "boast in Jehovah!" To *boast* is "to speak of or assert with excessive pride." Normally, it has to do with a display of pride in oneself. However, in the case of *Hallelujah!* it means a display of pride or an assertion of glory and honor in the Lord. So then, whenever we say "Hallelujah!" we are asserting "let's give glory and praise to the Lord . . . and none other!"

This explains why some versions of the Bible prefer to translate *Hallelujah!* "Praise the Lord!" That is what it means. Self is ignored. Magnifying the Lord is the single concern of these last five psalms. Whenever we say "Hallelujah!" let's realize what we are saying. During praise-less times, we are usually preoccupied with *ourselves*. We find it almost impossible to focus fully on *Yah-weh*.

Looking at Psalm 149 as a whole, I find three significant points of interest:

1. It is written to believers—godly ones, not carnal ones. In verses 1, 5, and 9, the *godly ones* are specifically mentioned.

2. It is written to *Jewish* believers. This becomes evident as you examine such terms as *Israel* (v. 2), *sons of Zion* (v. 2), *His people* (v. 4), and *the nations* (Gentiles, v. 7).

3. It falls into three sections. Each section has to do with certain times in which we are to praise our Lord: (a) verses 1–3, times of blessing; (b) verses 4–6, times of suffering; (c) verses 7–9, times of warfare.

IN TIMES OF BLESSING

Praise the Lord!
Sing to the Lord a new song,

And His praise in the congregation of the godly ones.
Let Israel be glad in his Maker;
Let the sons of Zion rejoice in their King.
Let them praise His name with dancing;
Let them sing praises to Him with timbrel and lyre. [vv. 1–3]

The songwriter gives us three commands as he discusses times of blessing. He tells us to sing (v. 1), to be glad (v. 2), and to praise His name (v. 3) when we are blessed by God. Let's look at each command and meditate upon what God is saying.

Sing

We are told to sing *a new song*. When God rewards us, He is pleased to hear us respond with fresh and spontaneous expressions of delight. We are to share this publicly "in the congregation of the godly ones." Often we openly share our times of stress and heartache—and we should—but seldom do we feel as free to share those occasions when His abundant blessings surround us.

Be Glad

Times of prosperity and/or promotion that God makes possible should never cause guilt. No reason for that. Be glad! Rejoice! Unfortunately, some in the Christian ranks have begun to believe that it is spiritual to suffer, but almost shameful to be made prosperous. However, let's never forget that our rejoicing should be directed toward Him who brought the blessings, and not ourselves or another. Psalm 75:6–7 makes that clear:

For not from the east, nor from the west,
Nor from the desert comes exaltation;
But God is the Judge;
He puts down one, and exalts another.

If it is you He has chosen to lift up and exalt, accept it humbly; rejoice in it without guilt! This brings us to the third command.

Praise

The third verse tells us, in effect, to really "let loose." Don't hold your praise to yourself; let it out! In the days of the psalmist, it was quite common for God's people literally to dance for joy and play on musical instruments when they were filled with praise. David danced in the street when the ark was brought back into the city of David (2 Sam. 6:12–15). Likewise, Miriam, Moses' sister, danced in praise of God after the Israelites crossed the Red Sea (Exod. 15:20–21). The dancing in Scripture was done out of praise in one's heart to God for His blessings and deliverance.

The whole point of these first three verses of Psalm 149 is that we are to enjoy our times of blessing in full measure. We are to give our Lord fresh, unrestrained exclamations of praise when He chooses to pour out His abundance upon us. Those are the times when it is easy to say, "Praise the Lord." However, we are also to *Praise Him in times of suffering.*

IN TIMES OF SUFFERING

> For [since] the Lord takes pleasure in His people;
> He will beautify the afflicted ones with salvation.
> Let the godly ones exult in glory;
> Let them sing for joy on their beds.
> Let the high praises of God be in their mouth.
> And a two-edged sword in their hand. [vv. 4–6]

I think it would help to begin verse 4 with "Since" rather than "For." This is permissible with the original language, and it helps to separate verse 4 from the preceding section, as I believe it should be.

God's Viewpoint (v. 4)

I notice two statements in verse 4 regarding the way God views those who are afflicted with suffering:

1. He takes pleasure in them. The Hebrew term is *rah-tzah*, meaning "to accept favorably, be pleased with, satisfied with." So often the one who is set aside feels completely unloved and useless—even rejected. He isn't contributing a thing because he can't. Not able to produce, he begins to feel as though he is nothing but a drag, a weary responsibility. That is why suffering is usually a praise-less grind! But this verse says quite the opposite! It says that God "accepts us favorably"—He is "pleased with us" even when we are laid aside and totally unproductive. That fact alone should encourage each one who is afflicted with pain and sidelined because of illness. You may be in a hospital room or alone at home. Take heart! God still accepts you and looks upon you with favor, even though you cannot produce anything at this present time.

2. He beautifies them. To be technical about it, the verse says that God "will beautify the afflicted ones with salvation" (deliverance). This is so true. When deliverance comes, when healing occurs, when the sunshine of hope splashes across the once-dismal room of the sufferer, beauty returns. The long facial lines of stress begin to fade, the light returns to the eyes, the whole countenance is lifted. God beautifies them!

In a broader, nontechnical sense, however, I want to suggest that God beautifies many who live long years *with* affliction. Some of the most beautiful people I have known are people whose lives have been scarred by disease, pain, and paralysis. Stationed upon their bed or limited to a chair, these "beautiful sufferers" have a radiance that shines like the quiet, faithful beam from a lighthouse across troubled waters. Often I go to minister to *them* . . . but I soon discover that the beauty of their lives ministers to *me!* Their attitude toward suffering prompts me to give praise to God.

Sufferer's Viewpoint (vv. 5–6)

The afflicted person is addressed in verses 5–6. Here God tells us how to handle times of suffering:

1. Exult (rejoice) in it
2. Sing about it (on the bed)

3. Praise God for it
4. Hold onto the two-edged sword through it

We have developed the first three already, but not the fourth. Hold fast to the sword! In other words, don't drop your defenses. Stay faithful to the Word of God—the sword of the Spirit (Eph. 6:17), the two-edged sword (Heb. 4:12).

Sickness and suffering have a tendency to weaken our faith if we fail to feed our thoughts with God's Word. Praise, like a fragrant blossom, wilts quickly. The sufferer is admonished to hold fast to the sword—good counsel. This is one of the reasons a visit with those who are ill should include sharing a portion of the living Book, the Bible. It helps the sufferer keep a firm grip on the two-edged sword. Finally, *we are to praise God in times of warfare.*

IN TIMES OF WARFARE

> To execute vengeance on the nations,
> And punishment on the peoples;
> To bind their kings with chains,
> And their nobles with fetters of iron;
> To execute on them the judgment written;
> This is an honor for all His godly ones.
> Praise the Lord! [vv. 7–9]

These final verses are the most difficult in the song to understand. As I stated earlier, it is important for us to interpret this psalm historically, with the believing Jew in mind. You see, the enemies of Israel were enemies of God, so Israel was trained to be a militant, aggressive force against wrong (they still are!) . . . to "execute vengeance on the nations and punishment on the peoples." This work of judgment was actually "written" (v. 9) in such passages as Deuteronomy 32:41–43; Joel 3; and Zechariah 14.

Practically, however, verses 7–9 exhort the Christian today to stand and fight against Satan and all his hosts of demons. Our warfare is not in the realm of the seen, but the unseen . . . not in the fleshly realm but the spiritual as we saw in our lengthy study of Psalm 91. This is precisely what 2 Corinthians 10:3–5 is saying:

> For though we walk in the flesh, we do not war according to the flesh, for the weapons of our warfare are not of the flesh, but divinely powerful for the destruction of fortresses. We are destroying speculations and every lofty thing raised up against the knowledge of God, and we are taking every thought captive to the obedience of Christ.

So then, let us be just as aggressive and militant against our spiritual foe as Israel was against her national foes. After all, "this is an honor for all His godly ones." To think that God would even allow us to be a part of His combat unit is an honor, indeed! May He be praised for equipping us for battle, empowering us for the fight, and encouraging us with the absolute promise of victory. Praise-less times are often times of demonic warfare . . . but the victory is ours! Read the following New Testament promises and rejoice.

> Therefore, my beloved brethren, be steadfast, immovable, always abounding in the work of the Lord, knowing that your toil is not in vain in the Lord. [1 Cor. 15:58]

> But thanks be to God, who always leads us in His triumph in Christ, and manifests through us the sweet aroma of the knowledge of Him in every place. [2 Cor. 2:14]

> And when you were dead in your transgressions and the uncircumcision of your flesh, He made you alive together with Him, having forgiven us all our transgressions, having canceled out the certificate of debt consisting of decrees against us and which was hostile to us; and He has taken it out of the way, having nailed it to the cross. When He had disarmed the rulers and authorities, He made a public display of them, having triumphed over them through Him. [Col. 2:13–15]

> Submit therefore to God. Resist the devil and he will flee from you. [James 4:7]

> You are from God, little children, and have overcome them; because greater is He who is in you than he who is in the world. [1 John 4:4]

CONCLUSION

Praise the Lord at all times! In times of blessing, praise Him! In times of suffering, praise Him! In times of warfare, praise Him! When we come to that enviable place in our Christian experience that we can honestly say "Praise the Lord!" in *every* situation—and genuinely mean it—we will have assimilated the full thrust of this magnificent hymn of praise—Psalm 149— and all the songs in Scripture. May that day come soon . . . and may it never end.

During the eighteenth century, Charles Wesley wrote numerous hymns. It has been estimated that during his lifetime he composed over eight thousand! "O for a Heart to Praise My God," one of his finest and oldest, has been put to the familiar tune of "O for a Thousand Tongues to Sing," another Wesley hymn. It is a fitting conclusion to our study of the songs in Scripture.

> O for a heart to praise my God,
>   A heart from sin set free,
> A heart that always feels Thy blood
>   So freely shed for me!
>
> A heart resigned, submissive, meek
>   My great Redeemer's throne;
> Where only Christ is heard to speak,
>   Where Jesus reigns alone.
>
> A heart in every thought renewed,
>   And full of love divine;
> Perfect, and right, and pure, and good,
>   A copy, Lord of Thine![19]

EFLECTIONS ON PRAISE-LESS TIMES

1. Do you remember the literal meaning of "Hallelujah"? Let's give it a whirl:

   hah-lale: _____

   Yah-weh: _____

   Put together: _____

2. What are the most common "praise-less" grinds in your life? Be specific. See if you can discover a pattern. Talk it over this week with close friends or a minister.

3. Whenever you encounter either a period of suffering or a time of warfare (as we saw in Psalm 149), just quietly utter, "Praise You, Lord!" and focus fully on Him. It can make an amazing difference. Furthermore, your countenance will be lifted up!

Can you believe it?

If you have been following the game plan I suggested at the beginning of Book I —taking one reading per week— we have already traveled three-fourths of the way through the year together. And what a journey it has been!

We began with thirteen weeks in the songs of Scripture, followed by a second section of the next thirteen weeks in the sayings of Scripture. We discovered that by balancing our time in the Psalms and the Proverbs, we could maintain our spiritual equilibrium a bit better. The songs seem to turn our attention toward God, while the sayings tend to address more of our horizontal needs and relationships.

Now that we have completed our second segment of studies in the songs, we have one final section in the sayings before we bring our yearlong journey to an end — thirteen more readings and applications of Solomon's wisdom in light of today.

So hang on! We're off again on our scriptural safari, looking for practical insights that will help us live beyond the daily grind. Before we know it, the winding trail of Truth will make its final bend, so pay close attention!

THE SAYINGS IN SCRIPTURE

WEEK 40
THROUGH
WEEK 52

The fear of the Lord is the
beginning of wisdom,
And the knowledge of the Holy
One is understanding.
For by me your days will be multiplied,
And years of life will be added to
you.   [9:10–11]

The Lord will not allow the righteous to
hunger,
But He will thrust aside the craving of
the wicked.   [10:3]

The way of the Lord is a stronghold to
the upright,
But ruin to the workers of
iniquity.   [10:29]

When a man's ways are pleasing to the
Lord,
He makes even his enemies to be at
peace with him.   [16:7]

Many are the plans in a man's heart,
But the counsel of the Lord, it will
stand.   [19:21]

The king's heart is like channels of water
in the hand of the Lord;
He turns it wherever He wishes.   [21:1]

THE GRIND OF
SUBMISSION TO
SOVEREIGNTY

At first glance the list of sayings on the previous page may appear more like a hodgepodge of random thoughts. A closer look, however, reveals a common theme—one we tend to forget or ignore. It is the theme of God's almighty sovereignty.

Since our generation is so hung up on human ingenuity and carnal cleverness, we tend to give people strokes that only God deserves.

- A battle is won . . . we hang medals on veterans.

- A degree is earned . . . we applaud the graduates.

- A sum of money is donated . . . we engrave contributors' names in bronze.

- An organization stays in the black through hard times . . . we give the CEO a bonus.

- A writer or scientist makes an outstanding contribution . . . we award the Pulitzer or Nobel prize.

- A sermon meets numerous needs . . . we thank the preacher.

There's nothing at all wrong with showing appreciation, just so we acknowledge the One who really deserves the maximum credit and give Him the greatest glory. But since He works out His will so silently (and often mysteriously), we feel a little spooky saying much about His almighty sovereignty.

Too bad. More needs to be said these days about God's sovereignty. Why? Because when so little is being said, man starts to strut his stuff. Look back at those timeless sayings from Solomon's pen. Read them slower this time.

Do you see what they are saying? God is in charge. Actually He is an unseen stronghold to the upright and an unseen obstacle in the way of the wicked (10:3, 29). He is *so* powerful that He can honor those who please Him by changing the attitudes of those who once felt enmity toward His followers (16:7). And get this: Once it is all said and done, after our plans have been hammered out, thought through, reworked, decided on, and distributed—it is ultimately *His* counsel that will stand.

That doesn't make you nervous, does it? You're not bothered by these comments about a doctrine that has become controversial, are you? Solomon didn't learn of God's sovereignty from John Calvin, remember; Calvin learned it from Scripture. Relax, this isn't simply "reformed doctrine," it is revelational doctrine. Frankly, I find it extremely comforting and enormously relieving. But for many (especially the hard-charging, do-it-yourself types) submission to sovereignty is an irksome daily grind. That's too bad.

Let's dig a little deeper into Proverbs 21:1:

> The king's heart is like channels of water in the hand of the Lord;
> He turns it wherever He wishes.

Immediately we can see it is a "comparative couplet" (see earlier discussion pp. 157–158 Book I). Something is compared to something else. Most comparative couplets end with the comparison and leave it at that. But this saying comes to a conclusion in what could be called the declarative part of the proverb . . . leaving the reader a timeless principle.

Observe the comparison: "The king's heart is like channels of water in the hand of the Lord." The Hebrew sentence doesn't

begin with "the king's heart" but rather with "like channels."
The Hebrew term translated *channels* is one that refers to small
irrigation ditches that run from a main source—a reservoir—
out into dry thirsty flatlands needing a cool drink. In other
words: "Like irrigation canals carrying water is the heart of the
king in Jehovah's hand. . . ."

What's the point? The king's heart (his inner being), the internal part of him that makes decisions, breathes out and commu-
nicates attitudes and policies, edicts and laws. As a result, he
may appear to be in charge, but the entire matter from start
to finish silently and sovereignly rests in the Lord's hand. The
sovereign Lord, not the king or *any other* monarch or leader,
qualifies to be the U.C. with U.A.—Ultimate Chief with Ultimate Authority.

How can anyone say such a thing, especially if the human
authority is an unbeliever? Well, just finish reading Solomon's
saying: "He [the Lord Himself] turns it wherever He wishes."
Literally, He "causes it to be bent wherever He is pleased." God
is calling the shots. Again, I ask you—Do you have struggles
with that? If so, then you will really churn over this:

> "But at the end of that period I, Nebuchadnezzar, raised my
> eyes toward heaven, and my reason returned to me, and I
> blessed the Most High and praised and honored Him who lives
> forever;
>
> For His dominion is an everlasting dominion,
> And His kingdom endures from generation to generation.
> And all the inhabitants of the earth are accounted as nothing,
> But He does according to His will in the host of heaven
> And among the inhabitants of earth;
> And no one can ward off His hand
> Or say to Him, 'What hast Thou done?'" [Dan. 4:34–35]

Those are the words of a powerful king who was describing
how God had worked him over prior to his coming full circle.

What is true of ancient kings is also true of modern bosses.
Your boss. Or anyone else who thinks he is in full control. Yes,

even you. God is ultimately going to have His way. You may decide to wrestle or attempt to resist, but I've got news for you; He's never met His match. He will win. He will have His way.

And just in case today is a high-level stress day when submitting to your sovereign Lord doesn't seem all that fair or fulfilling, take my advice: Do it anyway. You'll be glad later. Maybe sooner.

 **EFLECTIONS ON SUBMITTING TO SOVEREIGNTY**

1. Do some digging on your own this week. Find a couple or three reliable reference works and write out your own expanded definition of God's sovereignty. Begin with "Divine sovereignty is _____

   _____

   _____

   _____."

2. For the balance of the week, pick out two Bible characters whose lives were uniquely directed by God. Read up on both. *Joseph* is a beautiful example from the Old Testament. (Genesis 50:15–21 is a classic reference.) And from the New Testament, *Saul of Tarsus* is another worth examining. (Note especially Acts 9:1–20.) God's hand on Joseph's life illustrates how He can change a heart from resentment to forgiveness. His hand on Saul's life illustrates His sovereign ability to bring a proud, strong-willed type to his knees in utter humility.

3. This weekend, get alone. Find a quiet place where you can think. And pray. And reorder your life. Speak openly and audibly to the Lord and tell Him of your willingness to "lay down your arms." Acknowledge your stubborn streak. Express your desire to let Him have His way. Invite Him to take charge of each segment of your life. Yes, each one.

The hand of the diligent will rule,
But the slack hand will be put to
forced labor.   [12:24]

A slothful man does not roast his prey,
But the precious possession of a man is
diligence.   [12:27]

The soul of the sluggard craves and gets
nothing,
But the soul of the diligent is made
fat.   [13:4]

The way of the sluggard is as a hedge of
thorns,
But the path of the upright is a
highway.   [15:19]

He also who is slack in his work
Is brother to him who destroys.   [18:9]

Laziness casts into a deep sleep,
And an idle man will suffer
hunger.   [19:15]

The sluggard says, "There is a lion
outside;
I shall be slain in the streets!"   [22:13]

The sluggard says, "There is a lion in the
road!
A lion is in the open square!"
As the door turns on its hinges,
So does the sluggard on his bed.
The sluggard buries his hand in the dish;
He is weary of bringing it to his mouth
again.
The sluggard is wiser in his own eyes
Than seven men who can give a discreet
answer.   [26:13–16]

THE GRIND OF
LAZINESS

Many people live under the false impression that work is a curse. Some attempt to quote Scripture to verify their position that work was the sad consequence of Adam's fall in the Garden of Eden. Wrong!

Before sin ever entered the human race—while total innocence prevailed—Adam was assigned the task of cultivating the Garden (Gen. 2:15). Work is not a curse. The curse that followed the Fall had to do with the hassles—the thorn- and thistlelike irritations that now accompany one's work—not work itself. Work, alone, is a privilege, a challenge to indolence, an answer to boredom, and a place to invest one's energy . . . not to mention to provide for our physical needs.

Throughout the Bible we are encouraged to be people of diligence, committed to the tasks in life that need to be accomplished. Some, however, do not consider this a privilege, but a drag. For those folks the daily grind of laziness is an undeniable reality. For this entire week, therefore, let's snap on our zoom lens and focus on this practical plague.

Of all the Scriptures that address the issue of laziness, none are more eloquent than the sayings of Solomon. Among the terms he uses for the lazy, "sluggard" seems to be his favorite. When I trace my way through the Proverbs, I find no less than *six characteristics* of the sluggard.

1. The sluggard has trouble getting started:

How long will you lie down, O sluggard?
When will you arise from your sleep?
"A little sleep, a little slumber,
A little folding of the hands to rest"—
And your poverty will come in like a vagabond,
And your need like an armed man. [6:9–11]

You may remember that in Book I we spent a week on procrastination, so there is no need to repeat what was presented in that study. Nevertheless, there is no getting around it: laziness focuses on the obstacles, the excuses that loom large on the front end of a task. Those who are lazy just can't seem to roll up their sleeves and plunge in full bore.

2. The sluggard is restless: He (or she) may have desires, but the trouble comes in implementing them:

The soul of the sluggard craves and gets nothing,
But the soul of the diligent is made fat. [13:4]

The desire of the sluggard puts him to death,
For his hands refuse to work;
All day long he is craving,
While the righteous gives and does not hold back. [21:25–26]

It is not uncommon for the lazy to be extremely skilled, creative people. They can talk and dream and even sketch out the game plan, but the discipline of pursuit is lacking. As we just read, the "craving" goes on "all day long," but little gets accomplished. When it comes to the sluggard's getting off dead center and getting the job done, forget it.

3. The sluggard takes a costly toll on others:

He also who is slack in his work
Is brother to him who destroys. [18:9]

That last word pulsates with liabilities. A lazy employee doesn't simply hold an organization back, he *destroys* its motivation and drive. A lazy player doesn't just weaken the team, he *destroys* its spirit, its will to win. A lazy pastor doesn't merely limit a church, he *destroys* its excitement, its passion to win souls and meet needs. Before long, everyone must do more to compensate for the sluggard's negative influence.

4. The sluggard is usually defensive:

> The sluggard is wiser in his own eyes
> Than seven men who can give a discreet answer. [26:16]

Can't you just hear it . . . all those rationalizing comments? Unfortunately, it is this clever ability to cover up or explain away that keeps the lazy person from coming to terms with reality.

5. The sluggard is a quitter:

> A slothful man does not roast his prey,
> But the precious possession of a man is diligence. [12:27]

In this saying, there is the telltale mark of laziness: an absence of thoroughness.

- He likes to catch fish, but not to clean them.

- He loves to eat, but don't expect him to help with the dishes.

- He can add a room onto the house, but getting it painted is another story.

He'd rather sleep than work; he'd rather focus on why something can't be helped . . . then blame the government for not caring (see Prov. 19:15).

6. The sluggard lives by excuses:

> The sluggard says, "There is a lion outside;
> I shall be slain in the streets!" [22:13]

That saying always makes me smile. Those lions in the street are nothing more than a fertile imagination gone to seed. The "lion" returns . . .

The sluggard says, "There is a lion in the road!
A lion is in the open square!"
As the door turns on its hinges,
So does the sluggard on his bed.
The sluggard buries his hand in the dish;
He is weary of bringing it to his mouth again. [26:13–15]

If it weren't so tragic, the analogy of a sluggard on a bed resembling a door on a hinge would be hilarious!

No one ever automatically or instantaneously overcame laziness. If this happens to be one of your daily grinds, today is the best day to start a new direction. The best place to start is by admitting it if you are lazy . . . stop covering it up. I dare you!

A young fellow rushed into a gas station to use the pay phone. The manager overheard his telephone conversation as he asked:

"Sir, could you use a hardworking, honest young man to work for you?" [pause] "Oh . . . you've already got a hardworking, honest young man? Well, thanks anyway!"

The boy hung up the phone with a smile. Humming to himself, he began to walk away, obviously happy.

"How can you be so cheery?" asked the eavesdropping service-station manager. "I thought the man you talked to already had someone and didn't want to hire you."

The young fellow answered, "Well, you see I *am* the hard-working young man. I was just checking up on my job!"

If you called your boss, disguised your voice, and asked about *your* job, what do you think would be the boss's answer?

EFLECTIONS ON LAZINESS

1. Go back over that list of six characteristics. Spend enough time on each to see yourself mirrored in the scene. Which two represent your greatest area(s) of weakness? Admit them in writing:

   a. _____

   b. _____

2. Now that you have identified your style, spell out a game plan for correcting the tendency to be lazy. Be specific, practical, and realistic. Begin your strategy with such words as: "Today, I will begin to . . ." or "From now on, I am going to . . ."

3. Do you happen to have a lazy acquaintance who holds you back? Frequently, an unhealthy or unwholesome association will give us just the excuse we need to settle for too many limitations. Do you really need to spend that much time with him (or her)? If you do, be honest and confront the problem. Ask the person either to join you in a strategy to change or to step aside so you can.

PROVERBS

If you are slack in the day of distress,
Your strength is limited.   [24:10]

Two things I asked of Thee,
Do not refuse me before I die:
Keep deception and lies far from me,
Give me neither poverty nor riches;
Feed me with the food that is my portion,
Lest I be full and deny Thee and say,
   "Who is the Lord?"
Or lest I be in want and steal,
And profane the name of my
   God.   [30:7–9]

THE GRIND OF IMBALANCE

The longer I live the more I realize the ease with which we can slip into extremes. I see it all around me and sometimes, to my own embarrassment, I find it in myself. A major prayer of mine as I grow older is, "Lord, keep me balanced!"

— We need a balance between work and play (too much of either is unhealthy and distasteful).

— We need a balance between time alone and time with others (too much of either takes a toll on us).

— We need a balance between independence and dependence (either one, all alone, leads to problems).

— We need a balance between kindness and firmness,
between waiting and praying, working and obeying,
between saving and spending,
between taking in and giving out,
between wanting too much and expecting too little,
between warm acceptance and keen discernment,
between grace and truth.

For many folks, the struggle with imbalance is not an annual conflict—it's a daily grind.
Solomon mentions one kind of test: adversity.

> If you are slack in the day of distress,
> Your strength is limited. [Prov. 24:10]

When things are adverse, survival is our primary goal. Adversity is a test on our resiliency, our creativity. Up against it, we reach down deep into our inner character and we "gut it out." We hold up through the crisis by tapping into our reservoir of inner strength.

But another far more subtle test is the opposite extreme: prosperity—when things begin to come easy, when there's plenty of money, when everybody applauds, when we get all our ducks in a row and the gravy starts pouring in. Now *that's* the time to hang tough! Why? Because in times of prosperity things get complicated. Integrity is on the block. Humility is put to the test. Consistency is under the gun. Of the two, I'm convinced prosperity is a much greater test than adversity. It is far more deceptive.

The one who wrote the following sayings understood all this much better than we. Listen to his wise counsel, actually a prayer:

> Two things I asked of Thee,
> Do not refuse me before I die:
> Keep deception and lies far from me,
> Give me neither poverty nor riches;
> Feed me with the food that is my portion,
> Lest I be full and deny Thee and say, "Who is the Lord?"
> Or lest I be in want and steal,
> And profane the name of my God. [30:7–9]

The man had lived enough years and seen enough scenes to boil his petition down to two specifics:

1. Keep me from deceiving and lying.
2. Give me neither too little nor too much.

It is that second request that intrigues us, isn't it? That is the one he amplifies. Why does he resist having too little? There would be the temptation to steal. Whoever doubts that has never looked into the faces of his own starving children. At that moment, feeding them could easily overrule upholding some high-and-mighty principle. Adversity can tempt us to profane the name of our God.

And why does he fear possessing too much? Ah, there's the sneaky one! It's *then*—when we're fat-'n'-sassy—that we are tempted to yawn at sacred things and think heretical thoughts like, *God? Aw, who really needs Him?* Prosperity can tempt us to presume on the grace of our God.

Think it over all week long. The adversary of our souls is the *expert* of extremes. He never runs out of ways to push us to the limit . . . to get us so far out on one end we start looking freaky and sounding fanatical as we cast perspective to the winds.

The longer I live, the more I must fight the tendency to go to extremes . . . and the more I value balance.

EFLECTIONS
ON IMBALANCE

1. Let's do a little honest appraisal, okay? To help keep your appraisal on a fairly reliable footing, two things will be needed:

   a. Your calendar
   b. Your checkbook

   Looking through your *calendar,* do you find a balance or imbalance? Too many things going on or too little time with others? And while you're looking, when was the last time you got away for an overnight . . . just to be refreshed? Is your time being kept in balance?

   Next, go back over the last several months in your checkbook. Go ahead, take a look! Do your expenditures reflect balance or imbalance? Too much (or not enough) on yourself? How about God's part? Is the way you spend your money an indication of balance?

2. Adversity or prosperity . . . toward which extreme are you? How are you handling the pressures? Does anyone know—I mean someone who can really pray you through these testy waters? Try not to underplay or overreact to the battle. You would be wise to memorize Proverbs 30:7–9 this week.

3. Let me put it straight: Is Christ truly Lord? Being the Bulwark of Balance, He is eminently capable of escorting you through life's daily grinds, including this one. It may be essential (you decide) for you to set aside one hour this week and turn all the details of your life over to Him, including your calendar and your checkbook.

Wisdom shouts in the street,
She lifts her voice in the
  square;
At the head of the noisy
  streets she cries out;
At the entrance of the gates in the city,
  she utters her sayings;
"How long, O naive ones, will you love
  simplicity?
And scoffers delight themselves in
  scoffing,
And fools hate knowledge?"   [1:20–22]

"Because they hated knowledge,
And did not choose the fear of the Lord.
They would not accept my counsel,
They spurned all my reproof.
So they shall eat of the fruit of their own
  way,
And be satiated with their own devices.
For the waywardness of the naive shall
  kill them,
And the complacency of fools shall
  destroy them."   [1:29–32]

THE GRIND OF OPPOSITION

By opposition, I am not referring to external resistance from others but to internal resistance within one's self. I'm not talking about our encounters with someone or something else that withstands our efforts. What I have in mind is how we personally withstand or resist the things of God—His leading, His reproofs, His will, His wisdom. Some are so given to internal opposition that they regularly fail to learn the lessons Truth attempts to teach. While others glean God's message and follow His principles, many spurn His ways. You may find yourself in that latter category these days.

As a pastor, I have been amazed at the difference among Christians when it comes to acceptance of instruction. Some never seem to learn. While there are always those who are sensitive and open to spiritual things—in fact, a few can't seem to get enough!—there are those who are exposed to the same truths year after year, but they fail to soak in. Not until I came across three types of individuals in the sayings of Scripture did I understand why. All three have the same thing in common—they are people of opposition, but they oppose in different ways.

The Simple

The "simple" are called "naive ones" by Solomon. The Hebrew *pah-thah* means "to be spacious, wide." In noun form it is frequently translated "door, entrance." It is the idea of being completely open, believing every word, easily misled, even enticed . . . an easy prey to deception. The naive are susceptible to evil and wide open to any opinion. They are usually inadequate when it comes to coping with life's complexities, especially if it requires a great deal of mental effort.

Reading through Proverbs, I find that the simple:

—are insensitive to danger or evil:

> For at the window of my house
> I looked out through my lattice,
> And I saw among the naive,
> I discerned among the youths,
> A young man lacking sense,
> Passing through the street near her corner;
> And he takes the way to her house,
> In the twilight, in the evening,
> In the middle of the night and in the darkness. [7:6–9]

> Suddenly he follows her,
> As an ox goes to the slaughter . . . [7:22a]

—do not envision the consequences:

> "Whoever is naive, let him turn in here,"
> And to him who lacks understanding she says,
> "Stolen water is sweet;
> And bread eaten in secret is pleasant."
> But he does not know that the dead are there,
> That her guests are in the depths of Sheol. [9:16–18]

—are gullible . . . they lack caution:

> The naive believes everything,
> But the prudent man considers his steps. [14:15]

—fail to learn . . . they plunge in again and again!

> The prudent sees the evil and hides himself,
> But the naive go on, and are punished for it. [22:3]

The Scoffer

Here is a person quite different from the simple. The scoffer "delights in his scoffing." The Hebrew term *lootz* means "to turn aside, to mock." It is the thought of rejecting with vigorous contempt . . . to refuse and to show disdain or disgust for spiritual truth. Back in Book I, during our very first week together, we read God's warning against sitting "in the seat of scoffers" (Ps. 1:1); so this is not our first encounter with those who sneer at the sacred.

Our response is to "whip 'em into shape," to apply a lot of intense discipline so they will stop scoffing. More than likely, that's wasted effort. Solomon reminds us:

> He who corrects a scoffer gets dishonor for himself.
> And he who reproves a wicked man gets insults for himself.
> Do not reprove a scoffer, lest he hate you,
> Reprove a wise man, and he will love you. [9:7–8]

This explains why all these fall under the general heading of "the opposition." The scoffer won't listen to words of correction. He vigorously opposes it.

> A wise son accepts his father's discipline,
> But a scoffer does not listen to rebuke. [13:1]

Nor will he (or she) appreciate our attempts to bring about a change.

> A scoffer does not love one who reproves him,
> He will not go to the wise. [15:12]

The Fool

The Hebrew root term for fool is *kah-sal*, meaning "to be stupid, dull." Its Arabic counterpart means "to be sluggish, thick, coarse." Don't misunderstand. The fool has the capacity to reason, he just reasons wrongly. Fools are absolutely convinced of one thing: they can get along quite well *without* God. Scripture reserves some of its severest rebukes for fools.

- Fools traffic in wickedness . . . they play with it.

  Doing wickedness is like sport to a fool;
  And so is wisdom to a man of understanding. [10:23]

- Fools place folly on display . . . they flaunt it.

  Every prudent man acts with knowledge,
  But a fool displays folly. [13:16]

- Fools arrogantly "let it all hang out."

  A wise man is cautious and turns away from evil,
  But a fool is arrogant and careless. [14:16]

Strong words! Nevertheless, they need to be heard. They also help explain why the resistance factor is so obvious among some. Resistance is not only real to some and common among humanity in general, but it may also be *your* personal daily grind. If so, this is the week to come to terms with it. And that is true even if you have little insignificant-looking areas of opposition in only a few quiet corners of your heart. Few things please our Lord more than a teachable spirit.

Do you possess one?

 **EFLECTIONS ON OPPOSITION**

1. See if you can, in your own words, define the three types of individuals we found mentioned in the sayings of Scripture:

   • The simple _____

   _____

   • The scoffer _____

   _____

   • The fool _____

   _____

   Can you think of a biblical example of each?

2. Which one represents an area of struggle for you? Can you call to mind a recent occasion that illustrates this fact? If you have children, can you see this same trait being played out in one (or more) of them? Spend some time thinking how you can help counteract that tendency.

3. Since no one else (according to Proverbs) seems that effective when it comes to changing the simple, the scoffer, or the fool, the responsibility for such rests with the individuals themselves. What are some things you can *do* personally to turn the tide? Aside from wishing and praying, describe two or three action steps that will begin to move you from the ranks of opposition. When do you plan to start?

Wine is a mocker, strong drink
a brawler,
And whoever is intoxicated
by it is not wise.   [20:1]

Who has woe? Who has sorrow?
Who has contentions? Who has
   complaining?
Who has wounds without cause?
Who has redness of eyes?
Those who linger long over wine,
Those who go to taste mixed wine.
Do not look on the wine when it is red,
When it sparkles in the cup,
When it goes down smoothly;
At the last it bites like a serpent,
And stings like a viper.
Your eyes will see strange things,
And your mind will utter perverse
   things.
And you will be like one who lies down
   in the middle of the sea,
Or like one who lies down on the top of a
   mast.
"They struck me, but I did not become ill;
They beat me, but I did not know it.
When shall I awake?
I will seek another drink."   [23:29–35]

THE GRIND OF
ADDICTION

I smile inside every time I hear someone say the Bible is irrelevant. Right away, I know that person is not well acquainted with the pages of God's Book. As one who has been a student of Scripture for over three decades, I am still occasionally stunned at how up-to-date and on target it really is.

Take the daily grind of addiction—for many today, a grim reality. Is there any subject of greater relevance than this one? And yet, centuries ago, when the Lord was directing His messengers to record His truth, this was a subject He chose not to overlook. Here we sit on the verge of the twenty-first century swarming with evidence of modern technology everywhere we turn, yet the ancient sayings of a long-ago writer speak with fresh relevance.

His collection of wise sayings includes pertinent words and warnings for all who may be tempted by the taste of alcohol or, to apply it further, by the allurements of some drug. Chemical abuse is no longer in hiding, whispered about by a select body of professionals behind closed doors. It is now out of the closet. Support groups in communities, colleges, and churches are available all across the country. They have people in them who don't scold or scream, preach or moralize . . . they offer support. They take time. They encourage. They care. Most of them have been through the hellish nightmare of addiction, so they understand what it feels like to be trapped, held captive by a bottle, a pill, a snort, an injection . . . or even food.

Substance abuse is no longer limited to the sleazy back alley. It's now in the high-rise owned by the high roller, in nice homes where small children play, in efficient offices where business is transacted, in military barracks where boredom is high, and on professional sports teams where competition is fierce and where money is plentiful. It's even in prisons where men and women serve time.

Perhaps there's an addiction to some substance in your life as well. You may be an upstanding and admired citizen—you may even be active in your community or church—but the *real* you is dependent on a drink or a "high" you get from some other substance. You, of all people, understand the warnings of Solomon: "Wine is a mocker" and "At the last it bites like a serpent." You hardly need to be reminded that as a result of taking it in, "Your eyes will see strange things, and your mind will utter perverse things." Yet, in spite of the humiliation and the embarrassment, you're back at it the next day (as Solomon describes it), again thinking "I will seek another drink." To call this incredible craving a "daily grind" is to put it mildly. It is more like a devastating grip you simply cannot conquer . . . an evil force beyond your ability to control.

I would not be foolish enough to suggest that within a week's time you will be free—certainly not. (There are a few who testify of overnight transformations, but they are the exception, not the norm.) However, I can assure you of this: Within a week you can be moving in a new direction. No addiction—I repeat: NO addiction—is more powerful than the power of the Almighty. Never forget that His power stills storms and heals diseases and casts out demons. In fact, it is the same power that once raised Jesus from the dead.

You think His power can't handle your addiction? You're convinced that you are beyond hope? You're not sure this God who brought His Son back from beyond can give you the strength you need to say "No" one day at a time? Get serious! Then read the following verses and rejoice with new hope:

Fear not, for I am with you. Do not be dismayed. I am your God. I will strengthen you; I will help you; I will uphold you with my victorious right hand. [Isa. 41:10, TLB]

But remember this—the wrong desires that come into your life aren't anything new and different. Many others have faced exactly the same problems before you. And no temptation is irresistible. You can trust God to keep the temptation from becoming so strong that you can't stand up against it, for he has promised this and will do what he says. He will show you how to escape temptation's power so that you can bear up patiently against it. [1 Cor. 10:13, TLB]

In our church in Fullerton, we have a ministry for those who struggle with chemical abuse. The name of this wonderful support group is "Lion Tamer's Anonymous." The stories of recovery that emerge from the ranks of those courageous folks are nothing short of thrilling.

I recall one that involved a married couple with several small children. Both parents were addicted to cocaine. It was not unusual for them to be high on the drug for a day or two each weekend. Thanks to the compassionate and gentle, yet firm, determination of a few caring friends in our Lion Tamer's group, this couple has found ways to "escape temptation's power."

If some addiction has become your daily grind, I urge you to face it head-on . . . up-front. Do whatever is needed to break its grip. Yes, *whatever*.

EFLECTIONS ON ADDICTION

1. To begin with, write out *The Living Bible* paraphrase of the two verses of Scripture you just read (Isaiah 41:10 and 1 Corinthians 10:13) on a three-by-five card or a small slip of paper. Keep it near your bed at night, on the table near where you sit to watch television, beside you where you work, and on the dashboard of the car you drive. Read the statements every day. By the end of the week, have them committed to memory. Personalize the two scriptures by inserting *your* name in place of "you" and "your."

2. Stop trying to ignore or excuse your addiction. As I mentioned a moment ago, face it. Confront the truth. Finish this sentence:

   I, _____, am addicted to _____.
      (your name)   (substance)

   Nobody ever began to overcome any habit who failed to admit it was true . . . so start there.

3. You need not only the prayers of others, but you need practical support as well. Locate a group, a professional hands-on person, or find a reliable clinic that specializes in helping people deal with your addiction. Reach out and admit your need for assistance. You may need to be hospitalized or go through an extensive program as an initial plan to get started. For sure, you must be accountable to a small group of caring individuals— preferably those who will not only help you work through your battle but those who will also support your faith. However, you must make the first move. Make it *today.* Good for you!

He who mocks the poor
    reproaches his Maker;
He who rejoices at calamity
    will not go
    unpunished. [17:5]

Do not rejoice when your enemy falls,
And do not let your heart be glad when
    he stumbles;
Lest the Lord see it and be displeased,
And He turn away His anger from him.

Do not fret yourself because of evildoers,
Or be envious of the wicked;
For there will be no future for the evil
    man;
The lamp of the wicked will be put
    out. [24:17–20]

If your enemy is hungry, give him food
    to eat;
And if he is thirsty, give him water to
    drink;
For you will heap burning coals on his
    head,
And the Lord will reward
    you. [25:21–22]

THE GRIND OF REVENGE

Have you spent much time around someone who is eaten up with the cancer of revenge—someone who is nursing an attitude of resentment? It is a tragic thing to witness. These folks are walking time bombs. Festering bitterness searches for and usually finds ways to explode. Often, those who suffer the brunt of another's revenge are innocent bystanders. They just happen to be in the way when the volcano erupts. Since revenge fuels such an enormous and uncontrollable fire, it is a wonder more aren't hurt by it. It may be a popular reaction, but it is not a solution.

I think Sir Francis Bacon had the right idea when he said:

> Revenge is a kind of wild justice; which the more man's nature runs to, the more ought law to weed it out. . . . certainly, in taking revenge a man is but even with his enemy; but in passing over it, he is superior, for it is a prince's part to pardon.

It is possible that revenge happens to be your personal daily grind. If so, trust me, you have a lot of company in that struggle. It is a common ailment woven into the fabric of universal humanity. There isn't a culture where revenge isn't found. But that doesn't excuse it! This is the week to expose revenge in all its ugliness. Like a tumor that will ultimately turn a healthy body into a corpse if it is ignored, this disease-carrying growth must be removed. The sooner, the better.

But how? Here's where God's Word comes to our rescue! First, we must do something that is painful within ourselves— we must forgive our enemy; and second, we must do something that is profitable for our "enemy."

FORGIVE YOUR ENEMY

First things first. The revenge clings tenaciously within us because we have not forgiven the other person. Sounds simple—too simple—doesn't it? How do I know I've not forgiven someone else? I rejoice at the thought of calamity striking him or her . . . but Solomon's saying declares that such an attitude "will not go unpunished." The stinging acid of resentment will eat away at my own inner peace. Furthermore, by our rejoicing when our enemy falls, we somehow hold back God's anger (Prov. 24:17–18). In some mysterious way, the Lord's taking vengeance on our behalf is connected to our releasing all of that to Him. By our refusing to forgive, revealed in our looking with delight on the offender's calamity, we hinder the divine process. Vengeance is God's work, but it awaits our releasing it to Him.

> "'Vengeance is Mine, and retribution,
> In due time their foot will slip;
> For the day of their calamity is near,
> And the impending things are hastening upon them.'
> For the Lord will vindicate His people,
> And will have compassion on His servants;
> When He sees that their strength is gone,
> And there is none remaining, bond or free." [Deut.
>   32:35–36]

Because that is true, all thought of our taking revenge must be put to bed. When we do, we "leave room [or give a place] for the wrath of God" (Rom. 12:19) to go to work. Read the following slowly and very carefully:

Never pay back evil for evil to anyone. Respect what is right in the sight of all men. If possible, so far as it depends on you, be at peace with all men. Never take your own revenge, beloved, but leave room for the wrath of God, for it is written, "Vengeance is Mine, I will repay, says the Lord." [Rom. 12:17–19]

So much for the first part: forgive, forgive, forgive!

SHOW KINDNESS TOWARD YOUR ENEMY

Now then, the second step proves the validity of our forgiveness . . . we do something beneficial on behalf of the one we once resented.

> If your enemy is hungry, give him food to eat;
> And if he is thirsty, give him water to drink;
> For you will heap burning coals on his head,
> And the Lord will reward you. [Prov. 25:21–22]

• Your now-forgiven enemy is hungry? Provide a nice meal.

• Your now-forgiven enemy is thirsty? Prepare a cool drink.

"That's easy enough," you say. "But what does all this mean about heaping burning coals on his head?"

In ancient days, homes were heated and meals were fixed on a small portable stove, somewhat like our outside barbecue grills. Frequently, a person would run low on hot coals and would need to replenish his supply. The container was commonly carried on the head. So as the individual passed beneath second-story windows, thoughtful people who had extra hot coals in their possession would reach out of the window and place them in the container atop his head. Thanks to the thoughtful generosity of a few folks, he would arrive at the site with a pile of burning coals on his head and a ready-made fire for cooking and keeping warm. "Heaping burning coals on someone's head" came to be a popular expression for a spontaneous and courteous act one person would voluntarily do for another.

The saying was still popular in the New Testament era, since Paul referred to it in a context very similar to the ones we've been considering in the sayings of Solomon.

"But if your enemy is hungry, feed him, and if he is thirsty, give him a drink; for in so doing you will heap burning coals upon his head." Do not be overcome by evil, but overcome evil with good. [Rom. 12:20–21]

I find it interesting that the only two places in Scripture where this custom is mentioned are in identical settings: demonstrating kindness toward someone who was once an offender—an enemy. That is worth some thought.

Equally significant is Paul's concluding remark. Instead of being "overcome by evil" (that's what happens when the cancer of revenge continues to spread its tentacles), we are told to "overcome evil with good."

The daily grind of revenge will continue to siphon our peace, our joy, and our love until we forgive—and I mean *completely* forgive—and ultimately prove our forgiveness through acts of kindness, courtesy, and thoughtfulness.

 EFLECTIONS
ON REVENGE

1. Do you have someone's face on the dart board of your mind? Be honest, now . . . 'fess up! Have you been entertaining thoughts of revenge toward another individual? Do you smile with cruel cynicism when you read the popular bumper sticker: "I don't get mad . . . I get even." As is true of all other transgressions, confession is the first step toward cleansing. Are you willing to admit to yourself and to the Lord that you've looked forward to the day when calamity would strike that person?

2. This is the week to work through whatever it takes to get rid of your secret. The ugly tumor of revenge *must* come out. If you can't seem to handle the surgical procedure alone, call for help. A minister, a priest, a counselor, a friend, a family member, a teacher—somebody who will not only hear you but help you. You'll need to talk it through (remember Proverbs 20:5 which we considered in the second section of Book I?) and hammer out a way to find peace within. Call on the Lord for His help. Take your time. Do a thorough job of cleaning all the corruption out of the wound. Don't be surprised if tears flow.

3. When the week has come to an end, begin to think of a way to "heap burning coals" on the head of that person. It may be in the form of a kind letter you write. Perhaps you could put in a good word for him (or her). Or send a gift—something tangible. Don't fake it. If you cannot pull it off with a pure motive, wait. The time will come when you will have an opportunity to do so.

Do not envy a man of violence,
And do not choose any of his
  ways.
For the crooked man is an
  abomination to the Lord;
But He is intimate with the
upright.   [3:31–32]

For jealousy [envy] enrages a man,
And he will not spare in the day of
  vengeance.
He will not accept any ransom,
Nor will he be content though you give
  many gifts.   [6:34–35]

A tranquil heart is life to the body,
But passion [envy] is rottenness to the
  bones.   [14:30]

Do not let your heart envy sinners,
But live in the fear of the Lord always.
Surely there is a future,

And your hope will not be cut off.
Listen, my son, and be wise,
And direct your heart in the
way. [23:17–19]

———————

Do not be envious of evil men,
Nor desire to be with them;
For their minds devise violence,
And their lips talk of trouble. [24:1–2]

———————

Do not fret because of evildoers,
Or be envious of the wicked;
For there will be no future for the evil
man;
The lamp of the wicked will be put
out. [24:19–20]

———————

Wrath is fierce and anger is a flood,
But who can stand before jealousy
[envy]? [27:4]

———————

THE GRIND OF ENVY

Envy is one of the great enemies of inner peace. It steals contentment from the heart. Petrarch was so right when he said:

> Five great enemies to peace inhabit within us: avarice, ambition, envy, anger, and pride. If those enemies were to be banished, we should infallibly enjoy perpetual peace.

Envy is the desire to equal another in achievement or excellence or possessions. The ancients referred to it as a malignant or hostile feeling. Augustine lists it among "the passions [that] rage like tyrants and throw into confusion the whole soul . . . with storms from every quarter." He then describes such a soul as having an "eagerness to win what was not possessed. . . . Wherever he turns, avarice can confine him, self-indulgence dissipate him, ambition master him, pride puff him up, envy torture him, sloth drug him. . . ."[1]

An apt term: *torture.* Such is the toll envy takes on its victims.

Jealousy and *envy* are often used interchangeably, but there is a slight difference. Jealousy begins with full hands but is frightened or threatened by the loss of its plenty. It is the resistance to losing what one has, in spite of the struggle to keep it. Envy is not quite the same. Envy begins with empty hands, mourning what it *doesn't* have. In *Purgatorio,* Dante portrays it as "a blind beggar whose eyelids are sewn shut." One who is envious is unreasonable because he is sewn up within himself.

Such torture can scarcely be exaggerated. Jealousy wants

to possess what it already has; envy wants to have what another possesses.

Interestingly, both emerge in Scripture from the same Hebrew term *qua-nah,* which means "to be intensely red." It is descriptive of one whose face is flushed as a sudden surge of blood announces the rush of emotion. To demonstrate the grim irony of language, *zeal* and *ardor* and *envy* all come from a common linguistic root. The same emotion that "enrages a man" (Prov. 6:34) also floods him with zeal to defend his country or adore his wife and family.

On several occasions the sayings of Scripture include warnings against our being consumed by envy. As you read earlier, we are not to envy one who is violent, or to choose any of his ways. An abrupt burst of anger may get quick results, but in the long run, the long-term consequences far outweigh the initial benefits (Prov. 3:31–32). In fact, the cultivation of envy brings "rottenness to the bones" (Prov. 14:30).

I find it extremely significant that the most-often repeated warnings regarding envy have to do with our being envious of the sinner, of evil men and their wayward lifestyle (Prov. 23:17; 24:1, 19). That should not surprise us. A favorite unguarded mind game so many folks play is to imagine how stimulating it would be to live it up . . . to throw restraint to the winds and "let it all hang out." Face it, sin has its sensual and seasonal pleasures. They may be short-lived and passing (Heb. 11:25), but they're certainly not dull and boring!

Furthermore, the wicked appear to get away with murder. Haven't you noticed? They maneuver their way through life with relative ease, they get out of trouble by lying and cheating, they can own and drive whatever, live wherever, and con whomever they wish out of whatever they want. And it seems as though they usually get away with it! And all this without accountability or responsibility. If something gets to be a hassle, bail out of it! If somebody gets in the way, walk over him! When we compare that self-satisfying lifestyle to the disciplines of devotion and the restraints of righteousness, it doesn't take an advanced degree from Dartmouth to see how envy can creep in.

And while we're at it, envy isn't limited to inner tortures over the ungodly. We can be just as envious of our fellow Christians.

It happens so quickly! That age-old, red-face flush can happen in dozens of life's scenes:

- When we hear a more polished speaker
- When we watch a more capable leader
- When we visit a bigger church
- When we read a better book
- When we meet a more beautiful, thinner woman (or a more handsome or charming man)
- When we observe a more effective evangelist
- When we ride in a more luxurious car
- When we listen to a more popular singer

The envy-list has no end. Not even preachers are immune!

Perhaps *this* is your daily grind. It is possible that the grind is intensifying as your age is outrunning your accomplishments. There was once a time when you could push that feeling away and keep a lid on it as you stored it in your attic of future dreams. Hope kept it diffused. No longer.

The reality of truth refuses to let you push envy aside any longer. The fact is . . . you won't be able to have or own or enjoy most of the things you see and hear others enjoying. And it is robbing you of that "perpetual peace" as envy tortures you with its malignant whisperings. What is worse, instead of your being happy for the other person whom God has blessed, you are suspicious or resentful, maybe downright angry. "Envy," reminds Solomon, "enrages a man."

This is the week to come to terms with envy. How much more peaceful to be contented with our lot! How much better to "rejoice with those who rejoice"! A mark of maturity is the ability to appreciate another more gifted than we . . . to applaud another more honored than we . . . to enjoy another more blessed than we. Such a wholesome response underscores our confidence in and allegiance to the sovereignty of God, who "puts down one and exalts another" (Ps. 75:7).

All week long let's expose our inner struggle with envy to the Physician of our souls. Like revenge, envy is another tumor we dare not ignore. Let's invite the Physician's scalpel and allow Him to excise it. If ignored, envy can become a terminal illness of the soul.

EFLECTIONS ON ENVY

1. Before the week ends, get a Bible concordance and look up every reference in Scripture under the headings of "envy" and "envious." Read each verse you locate slowly and aloud. Let the Spirit touch your inner spirit with the full impact of His truth. It may hurt, but it will ultimately help bring healing.

2. Do a little analysis of *your* battle with envy. Does it spring most often from a comparison of material possessions? *Why?* Does it increase when you are around more educated or capable people? *Why?* Does it emerge when you think of "what might have been" in your own life? *Why?* Could it be that envy is at the root of your underlying critical spirit? Could this explain why you have become more suspicious of those whom God has chosen to bless? Since "jealousy [*qua-nah*] is as severe as Sheol [the grave]" (Song of Solomon 8:6), it can leave its victim immobilized. Talk to God about this.

3. This weekend, take a little extra time to turn your attention from others' achievements and blessings to your own. Count them one by one. Make a mental list of what the Lord has done *for* you and *through* you. Don't miss your years of service, your health, or your continued ability to be of help to others. Pray for contentment. Pray for healing from the plague of comparison. Pray for a grateful spirit. Finally, be big enough to pray for at least three other people who are being used by God in a greater or broader way than He has chosen to use you. Pray for their success, their continued effectiveness, and their protection from enemy attacks.

A man's discretion makes him
   slow to anger,
And it is his glory to overlook a
   transgression.   [19:11]

Deliver those who are being taken away
   to death,
And those who are staggering to
   slaughter, O hold them back.
If you say, "See, we did not know this,"
Does He not consider it who weighs the
   hearts?
And does He not know it who keeps your
   soul?
And will He not render to man according
   to his work?   [24:11–12]

To show partiality is not good,
Because for a piece of bread a man will
   transgress.   [28:21]

The righteous is concerned for the rights
    of the poor,
The wicked does not understand such
    concern.   [29:7]

There is a kind of man who curses his
    father,
And does not bless his mother.
There is a kind who is pure in his own
    eyes,
Yet is not washed from his filthiness.
There is a kind—oh how lofty are his
    eyes!
And his eyelids are raised in arrogance.
There is a kind of man whose teeth are
    like swords,
And his jaw teeth like knives,
To devour the afflicted from the earth,
And the needy from among
    men.   [30:11–14]

THE GRIND OF INTOLERANCE

Tolerance provides "wobble room" for those who can't seem to measure up. It also allows needed growing room for the young and the restless. It smiles rather than frowns on the struggling. Instead of rigidly pointing to the rules and rehearsing the failures of the fallen, it stoops and reaches out, offering fresh hope and acceptance.

Intolerance is the antithesis of all that I have just described. Unwilling to "overlook a transgression" (Prov. 19:11), it tightens the strings on guilt and verbalizes a lot of shoulds and musts. The heart of the intolerant has not been broken, not really. For many, it has become unbreakable, judgmental, without compassion.

Don't misunderstand; most of this lack of tolerance is not overt, but subtle. You can detect it in a look; it is not usually spoken. To draw upon Solomon's saying, instead of delivering those who are going under, those "staggering to slaughter," the intolerant excuse their lack of assistance by saying, "We did not know this" (Prov. 24:11–12). But the Lord knows better. The Lord is well aware of even the slightest spirit of partiality hidden in our hearts.

Is intolerance one of your daily grinds? Be honest; do you have difficulty leaving room for differing opinions or others who can't measure up? Could it be that you have tasted for so long the ecstasies of conquest that you've forgotten the agonies of defeat? I can think of any number of ways intolerance rears its head:

- The healthy can be impatient with the sickly.

- The strong have trouble adapting to the weak.

- The fleet do not do well with the slow.

- The productive lack understanding of the drudge.

- The wealthy can scarcely imagine the pain of being poor.

- The quick minds know nothing of the embarrassment of being a slow learner.

- The coordinated shake their heads at the awkward.

- The pragmatic criticize the philosophical.

- The engineer has little appreciation for the artist.

- The stable and secure haven't a clue on how to understand the fragile and fearful.

Karl Menninger wrote with keen perception:

> When a trout rising to a fly gets hooked on a line and finds himself unable to swim about freely, he begins with a fight which results in struggles and splashes and sometimes an escape. Often, of course, the situation is too tough for him.
>
> In the same way the human being struggles with his environment and with the hooks that catch him. Sometimes he masters his difficulties; sometimes they are too much for him. His struggles are all that the world sees and it naturally misunderstands them. It is hard for a free fish to understand what is happening to a hooked one.[2]

Perhaps you fall into the category of a "free fish." Having never felt the sting of a hook or the choking panic of being caught, you would do well to keep your pride in check! Solomon muses over certain kinds of people who are "pure in their own eyes," whose "eyelids are raised in arrogance." Interestingly, their teeth become swordlike, sharp as knives. And whom do they devour, according to the saying of Scripture? "The afflicted . . . the needy" (Prov. 30:14). Why, of course! The intolerant invariably choose to devour those they consider "beneath them."

This is an excellent time—all week long—to bring even the slightest intolerance that may be lurking in your life out in the open and place it before the Lord. Reflecting back on our study of Psalm 139, call to mind those last two verses, especially David's petition: "Search me, O God . . . And see if there be any hurtful way in me, / And lead me in the everlasting way." What a perfect occasion to talk with the Lord about your intolerance!

Before closing off our study, let's consider one more saying worth our examination:

> The generous man will be prosperous,
> And he who waters will himself be watered. [Prov. 11:25]

True, the initial interpretation of Solomon's words is related to being generous with one's money, but broaden it to include being generous of spirit—broad-shouldered and big-hearted. Such an individual will not be restrictive in spirit or demanding, but "generous" of soul. The good news is that the same will come back to him. Others, in turn, will be accepting and tolerant in return.

It may be hard for a free fish to understand what is happening to a hooked one, but it isn't completely impossible. Our Lord knew no sin, did no sin, had no sin. Although He was never "hooked," His heart went out to those who were ashamed of their sin. On one occasion He even stood in defense of a woman caught in the very act of adultery.

Remember His words of tolerance bathed so beautifully in grace? After shaming those self-appointed judges who were ready to stone her, He looked deeply into the fallen woman's eyes and gently reassured her, "Neither do I condemn you; go your way; from now on sin no more" (John 8:11). Not a hint of intolerance.

If intolerance has become a daily grind, it is imperative that you deal with it. I'm thinking not only of you but of others who suffer the blunt edge of your habit. Those around you who are forced to live with your rigidity would be relieved to know that you are aware of your problem and that you plan to ignore it no longer. This week could be a turning point for you.

EFLECTIONS
ON INTOLERANCE

1. Do your best to describe the contrast between tolerance and intolerance. Two clarifications need to be thought through:

   a. When does tolerance become wholesale permission? How far is too far?

   b. There must be times when intolerance is appropriate, since Jesus drove the moneychangers out of the temple. Name another time or two in Scripture when our Lord refused to give ground. What does that imply?

2. Is there someone you know who could use an arm around a shoulder, a word of encouragement, and a few hours of companionship? Perhaps this person didn't measure up to the expectations of you or others, or holds to a different opinion on a controversial subject, or recently went through a time of personal disappointment that took the wind out of his or her sails. Would you risk making contact? Reach out and demonstrate compassion on that person's behalf. Listen to where he or she is coming from. *Really* listen. Call to mind Solomon's counsel regarding our being slow to anger: "It is his glory to overlook a transgression" (Prov. 19:11). Model that this week. As you do, you may be allowed to witness genuine healing.

3. Finally, it is time for some reflection. Since it is true that intolerance and arrogance are often related, could it be

that you have forgotten those occasions when *you* blew it . . . when you were like that trout, hooked and unable to get free? For the next ten minutes, vividly recall the pain of feeling alone, ashamed, and misunderstood. Think of a person or two who laid aside all pride as he (or she) invested time and demonstrated compassion. Ask the Lord to give you the courage to do the same. Time may be more of the essence than you realize.

PROVERBS

F our things are small on the earth,
  But they are exceedingly wise:
  The ants are not a strong folk,
  But they prepare their food in the
    summer;
The badgers are not mighty folk,
Yet they make their houses in the rocks;
The locusts have no king,
Yet all of them go out in ranks;
The lizard you may grasp with the hands,
Yet it is in kings' palaces.   [30:24–28]

THE GRIND OF
EXCUSE-MAKING

Ants, badgers, locusts, and lizards . . . sounds like roll call for Noah's Ark! Or an advertisement for a new jungle movie. But no, these four creatures are discussed in Proverbs 30:24–28— another of those amazing sayings from Scripture that speaks volumes to us today.

According to the opening statement in verse 24, each of these four creatures is "small on the earth, but . . . exceedingly wise." Each represents a contrast. We shouldn't think that size means insignificance. Within each is a remarkable ability . . . and, likewise, a hidden peril. As we shall see, each teaches a lesson we would do well to learn.

The Ant

We have already looked at the ant in Book I, so there's no need to linger here over details already discussed. Suffice it to say that without some higher-ranking authority to drive them on, without great strength (one human foot can stomp several of them into oblivion!), the ant nevertheless works, works, works.

The Badger

This creature isn't big either, but it is extremely independent. A member of the weasel family, badgers grow to be not more than thirty inches long. They are sleek, low-slung (Corvette-like) ground dwellers. As nocturnal prowlers, they are seldom seen. Badgers are fierce fighters with powerful jaws; long, sharp teeth; and two-inch claws. Extremely rugged and resilient, they can whip creatures up to four times their size!

However, they are great at bluffing their opponents. A badger stands, snarling and arching its back . . . but at the precise moment it is about to get caught or chewed up and spit out, it suddenly retreats!

Here's how: Badgers are unlike all other animals whose hair is "set" in such a manner that it lies in only one direction. Remember how we can rub a cat "the wrong way" or do the same with a dog? Not so with a badger! Badgers' hair can go *both* ways. Its skin is so loose and its hair so thick and flexible that another creature can't get a good grip on it. This makes a badger the classic *escape artist!* When confronted, it may choose to fight. More often, however, (being clever) it will choose to retreat.

Now, we're beginning to uncover a clue in this list of small creatures. Both the ant, which can slip into an anthill, and the badger, which escapes when confronted, are good illustrations of one of man's (and woman's!) favorite indoor sports: *making excuses.* Some get so good at it, no one can get a grip on them. It may appear to be small and insignificant as grinds go, but excuse-making can take a heavy toll.

The Locust

We're getting smaller again. This insect is about the size of a grasshopper. They may have "no king" (unlike Canadian geese in flight or a pride of lions on a savanna which follow a definite leader); nevertheless, locusts are a team that can "go out in ranks." The gregarious locust swarm can wreck havoc on endless miles of crops. Interestingly, they can be mild and quiet, then suddenly become restless and irritable. They can turn in their moods and suddenly become violent, taking flight and traveling incredible distances.

Some swarms sound like a huge commercial jetliner overhead. And when they have finished with their attack on crops, every plant—every single plant—is stripped down to a barren, bleeding stalk, as if a fire had swept across the scene. One particular swarm was spotted as far as twelve hundred miles out at sea, flying northward from West Africa toward the British Isles. Another swarm covered a breadth of air space no less than two thousand square miles.

Amazing creature, the locust . . . and how moody! Quiet and placid, yet within moments, irritable and restless.

The Lizard

According to this saying, we're able to grasp the lizard with our hands, yet it is ever so slippery. The next thing we know, it winds up "in kings' palaces." How? Well, that's the lizard's secret; it's a master of disguises. It can blend in so perfectly with its background, no one even notices its presence. Operation camouflage. Slippery when grabbed, it squirts away, and to everyone's surprise, it shows up elsewhere in all its glory!

Ants, badgers, locusts, and lizards present a small but very clever message to all who live with the daily grind of excuse-making. We can easily escape, slip away, change our moods, and go right on without accepting or even acknowledging the confrontation. The devastation of living like that can be enormous. For example, those who continue to live financially irresponsible lives often wind up declaring bankruptcy. Or husbands and wives who prefer to overlook their part in marital conflicts go from one marriage to the next with little change in their habits. Unfortunately, making excuses never solves conflicts; it only postpones the consequences.

This is a good week to take a straight look at your tendency to dodge the hard questions . . . to ignore the warnings of a friend . . . to slip from the grip of one whose criticism may hurt at the moment, but later could prove extremely beneficial. Honestly now . . .

- Are you slippery?
- How about moody and evasive?

- Is it your tendency to bluff?
- Do you enjoy camouflage?
- Have you a favorite anthill of escape?
- Does confrontation annoy or frighten you?

All this week, work hard at coming to terms with your excuse-making lifestyle. Living beyond that daily grind starts with facing up to the truth.

EFLECTIONS ON EXCUSE-MAKING

1. Which creature are you more like:

   The ant? Why?
   The badger? In what way?
   The locust? How?
   The lizard? Explain.

2. Think of situations where you most often feel the need to slip away and run. See if you can detect a familiar pattern—a recurring scene. Now for the tough one: *Why?* What makes you so hard to nail down? Is there something to hide? Something you fear? Are you afraid to let others get close? What's the reason behind that pattern?

3. No relationships are more significant to our development than those of early childhood. It is during those years that we form our first habits in handling life situations. Reflect back:

   • Was your mother or father moody?
   • Was evasiveness permitted? Modeled?
   • Can you recall how confrontation may have been mishandled back then?
   • Were you taught to live without accountability?
   • Did you develop excuse-making in your early years?

   For the balance of this week, discuss this with a few friends. Be vulnerable. Talk openly about your ant-badger-locust-lizard makeup.

Honor the Lord from your
wealth,
And from the first of all your
produce;
So your barns will be filled with plenty,
And your vats will overflow with new
wine.   [3:9–10]

It is the blessing of the Lord that makes
rich,
And He adds no sorrow to it.   [10:22]

How much better it is to get wisdom than
gold!
And to get understanding is to be chosen
above silver.   [16:16]

The rich rules over the poor,
And the borrower becomes the lender's
slave.   [22:7]

Do not be among those who give pledges,
Among those who become sureties for
debts.

If you have nothing with which to pay,
Why should he take your bed from under
   you?   [22:26–27]

––––––––––––––––

Do not weary yourself to gain wealth,
Cease from your consideration of it.
When you set your eyes on it, it is gone.
For wealth certainly makes itself wings,
Like an eagle that flies toward the
   heavens.   [23:4–5]

––––––––––––––––

He who tills his land will have plenty of
   food,
But he who follows empty pursuits will
   have poverty in plenty.
A faithful man will abound with
   blessings,
But he who makes haste to be rich will
   not be unpunished.   [28:19–20]

––––––––––––––––

A man with an evil eye hastens after
   wealth,
And does not know that want will come
   upon him.   [28:22]

THE GRIND OF
FINANCIAL
IRRESPONSIBILITY

Few "grinds" in life are more nerve-racking and energy-draining than those growing out of financial irresponsibility. Many are the headaches and heartaches of being overextended. Great are the worries of those, for example, who continue to increase their indebtedness or spend impulsively or loan money to others indiscriminately.

These words may bring a sting to your conscience if they describe your situation. What's worse, they may describe where you have found yourself off and on for as long as you can remember. It may not bring much comfort to know that *you are not alone*, but there is perhaps no more common problem among Americans than this one. So common is it that places of business must protect themselves from this phenomenon by operating under strict guidelines. All this reminds me of a sign that made me smile. It hangs in a Fort Lauderdale restaurant:

IF YOU ARE OVER 80 YEARS OLD
AND ACCOMPANIED BY YOUR PARENTS,
WE WILL CASH YOUR CHECK

Some wag once described our times with three different definitions:

Recession: When the man next door loses his job.
Depression: When you lose your job.
Panic: When your wife loses her job.

Many families have reached the place where the wife's working is no longer an optional luxury, it's a necessity.

To the surprise of no one, the sayings of Scripture having to do with money are numerous. Long before Ben Franklin penned his wit and wisdom in *Poor Richard's Almanac,* Solomon's words had been around for centuries, available for all to read. And when you attempt to categorize them, you realize just how varied the subjects are that have to do with financial matters.

Solomon's sayings cover a broad spectrum, including getting money (earning and inheriting), releasing money (spending, squandering, loaning, and giving), investing money, saving money, and handling money wisely. The synonyms used in Scripture are many: money, wealth, riches, lending, borrowing, spending, giving, losing, silver, gold, plenty, abundance, want, poverty, and a half dozen others.

Having traced the subject through Solomon's sayings, I have discovered the following principles of money management. There are six of them.

1. Those who honor God with their money are blessed in return.

Honor the Lord from your wealth,
And from the first of all your produce;
So your barns will be filled with plenty,
And your vats will overflow with new wine. [3:9–10]

It is the blessing of the Lord that makes rich,
And He adds no sorrow to it. [10:22]

Adversity pursues sinners,
But the righteous will be rewarded with prosperity. [13:21]

I have said for years that you can tell much more about an individual's dedication to God by looking at that person's checkbook than by looking at his or her Bible. Again and again throughout Scripture, we read of the blessings God grants (not all of them tangible, by the way) to those who "honor the Lord" with their finances.

2. Those who make riches their passion lose much more than they gain.

Do not weary yourself to gain wealth,
Cease from your consideration of it.
When you set your eyes on it, it is gone.
For wealth certainly makes itself wings,
Like an eagle that flies toward the heavens. [23:4–5]

Can't you just picture the scene? For that reason I think it is appropriate that an eagle appears on much of our American currency! Who hasn't been tempted by some get-rich-quick scheme? And think of the thousands of people who are drawn into the broad and juicy appeal of the investors who promise they can make a killing for them on their "deal." Beware of words like "it's a once-in-a-lifetime" opportunity! When you hear such stuff, listen for the flapping of eagles' wings. And heed instead the wisdom of Solomon's words!

He who tills his land will have plenty of food,
But he who follows empty pursuits will have poverty in plenty.
A faithful man will abound with blessings,
But he who makes haste to be rich will not be unpunished.
    [28:19–20]

A man with an evil eye hastens after wealth,
And does not know that want will come upon him. [28:22]

3. Wisdom gives wealth guidance. If you have a choice between wisdom and wealth, count on it; *wisdom* is much to be preferred!

Take my instruction, and not silver,
And knowledge rather than choicest gold.
For wisdom is better than jewels;
And all desirable things can not compare with her. [8:10–11]

Riches and honor are with me,
Enduring wealth and righteousness.
My fruit is better than gold, even pure gold,
And my yield than choicest silver. [8:18–19]

How much better it is to get wisdom than gold!
And to get understanding is to be chosen above silver. [16:16]

Wisdom provides the recipient of increased finances with the restraints that are needed. Furthermore, it helps one maintain that essential equilibrium, for much wealth can be a heady trip. Since riches never made anyone honest or generous or discerning, wisdom must come aboard to steer our vessel around those disastrous shallow reefs. The reason for this brings us to a fourth principle of money management.

4. Increased riches bring increased complications. As I examine the biblical record, I find several such complications mentioned in the Book of Proverbs:

- A false sense of security

> The rich man's wealth is his fortress,
> The ruin of the poor is their poverty. [10:15]

> A rich man's wealth is his strong city,
> And like a high wall in his own imagination. [18:11]

- A sudden burst of many new "friends"

The poor is hated even by his neighbor,
But those who love the rich are many. [14:20]

Wealth adds many friends,
But a poor man is separated from his friend. [19:4]

A man of many friends comes to ruin,
But there is a friend who sticks closer than a brother. [18:24]

- The possibility of arrogance and pride

The poor man utters supplications,
But the rich man answers roughly. [18:23]

The rich man is wise in his own eyes,
But the poor who has understanding sees through him. [28:11]

- Increased moral temptations

Do not desire her beauty in your heart,
Nor let her catch you with her eyelids.
For on account of a harlot one is reduced to a loaf of bread,
And an adulteress hunts for the precious life.

Can a man take fire in his bosom,
And his clothes not be burned?
Or can a man walk on hot coals,
And his feet not be scorched? [6:25–28]

A man who loves wisdom makes his father glad,
But he who keeps company with harlots wastes his wealth. [29:3]

5. Money cannot buy life's most valuable possessions.

It is strange how so many live under the delusion that a fat bank account will make possible "the best things in life" when, in fact, it will provide no such thing. Don't misunderstand. There is nothing wrong with having wealth if it has been earned honestly and if one's perspective stays clear. However, "the good life" should not be equated with "the true life," which Paul calls "life indeed" (1 Timothy 6:19). Money will only buy things that are for sale . . . and happiness or a clear conscience or freedom from worry is not among them. Money can be used to purchase lovely and comfortable dwellings, pleasure vacations, and delightful works of art. But the priceless things in life are not for sale.

What are some of those priceless possessions?

- Peace

> Better is a little with the fear of the Lord,
> Than great treasure and turmoil with it. [15:16]

- Love

> Better is a dish of vegetables where love is,
> Than a fattened ox and hatred with it. [15:17]

- A good name . . . reputation and respect

> A good name is to be more desired than great riches,
> Favor is better than silver and gold. [22:1]

- Integrity

> Better is the poor who walks in his integrity,
> Than he who is crooked though he be rich. [28:6]

6. If handled wisely, money can be the means of great encouragement, but if mishandled, great stress.

Adversity pursues sinners,
But the righteous will be rewarded with prosperity.
A good man leaves an inheritance to his children's children,
And the wealth of the sinner is stored up for the righteous.
    [13:21–22]

Who can measure the encouragement our money can bring to others? If reared correctly, our children can benefit from and know the joy of receiving an inheritance from their parents. God's Word admonishes parents to provide for their families. Ministries of every kind are dependent upon the financial generosity of those who support them. The hungry can be fed, the poor can be clothed, the homeless can be sheltered, the abused can be comforted, the untaught can be educated . . . the list of possibilities is endless.

There is the flip side, however:

The rich rules over the poor,
And the borrower becomes the lender's slave. [22:7]

Do not be among those who give pledges,
Among those who become sureties for debts.
If you have nothing with which to pay,
Why should he take your bed from under you? [22:26–27]

This hardly needs to be explained. Pause over those key words . . . especially *slave*. No other term better describes the feeling of being financially irresponsible!

If this happens to be your "grind," let me encourage you to ignore it no longer. No more excuses! There are too many helpful books and reliable resources available for you to continue on in an irresponsible manner. Begin the process of change this week.

REFLECTIONS ON FINANCIAL IRRESPONSIBILITY

1. Select three or four from the many sayings about money matters you just read that speak most pointedly to you. Write them on separate three-by-five cards and commit them to memory. You might also tape one of them on the front of your checkbook! All week long reflect on the truth of what you are committing to memory. Use those truths in several conversations this week.
2. One of the most helpful, practical tools you can use in getting a handle on your money is a budget. Don't let the week draw to a close before you have established a simple and easy-to-follow personal budget. If you need help, ask someone you respect for advice. If that person cannot help, surely he or she can steer you in the right direction by referring you to help from another source. But don't let the week run its course before you have *written down* a realistic financial game plan you will put in motion.
3. There are several splendid books available today on the subject of handling money wisely. There are also seminars and conferences, plus audio and video tapes provided by reliable authorities in the field of finances. This week, take a giant step toward conquering the dragon of financial irresponsibility by doing one (or more) of three things:
   a. Purchase and begin reading a book on money management.
   b. Listen to a set of tapes on the subject.
   c. Look into a financial seminar that would best meet your need and make definite plans to attend.

An excellent wife, who can find?
For her worth is far above
jewels.
The heart of her husband trusts
in her,
And he will have no lack of gain.
She does him good and not evil
All the days of her life.
She looks for wool and flax,
And works with her hands in delight.
She is like merchant ships;
She brings her food from afar.
She rises also while it is still night,
And gives food to her household,
And portions to her maidens.
She considers a field and buys it;
From her earnings she plants a vineyard.
She girds herself with strength,
And makes her arms strong.
She senses that her gain is good;
Her lamp does not go out at night.
She stretches out her hands to the distaff,
And her hands grasp the spindle.
She extends her hand to the poor;
And she stretches out her hands to the
needy.
She is not afraid of the snow for her
household,

For all her household are clothed with
  scarlet.
She makes coverings for herself;
Her clothing is fine linen and purple.
Her husband is known in the gates,
When he sits among the elders of the
  land.
She makes linen garments and sells them,
And supplies belts to the tradesmen.
Strength and dignity are her clothing,
And she smiles at the future.
She opens her mouth in wisdom,
And the teaching of kindness is on her
  tongue.
She looks well to the ways of her
  household,
And does not eat the bread of idleness.
Her children rise up and bless her;
Her husband also, and he praises her,
  saying:
"Many daughters have done nobly,
But you excel them all."
Charm is deceitful and beauty is vain,
But a woman who fears the Lord, she
  shall be praised.
Give her the product of her hands,
And let her works praise her in the
  gates.   [31:10–31]

THE GRIND OF MOTHERHOOD

Without taking away from the joys, rewards, and those extra-special moments of motherhood, the daily tasks of that assignment can be *grinding!* Washing mounds of laundry; ironing; folding; cleaning; shopping; cooking; car pooling; being a referee, a coach, an encourager, a counselor, a cop; staying pretty; remaining tactful, lovable, compassionate, cheerful, responsible, balanced, and sane(!)—all have a way of making today's mothers feel strung out and spent. And it is all so daily . . . so relentlessly repetitive.

There is so much to know as well as to learn about this matter of being a good mother. It doesn't simply "just happen" once you have a child. It's as absurd to think that giving birth automatically makes you a good mother as it is to think that having a piano automatically makes you a good musician. There's an enormous amount of work to it, more than most will ever realize . . . (certainly more than most *husbands* realize, right?).

Among the eloquent sayings of Scripture is a most outstanding treatise on the mother's role. It is both profound and practical . . . full of wise counsel and strong encouragement. Anyone who reads this section realizes that God believes in the woman who gives her home the priority it deserves. He also sees her as a person, distinct and different from her husband, who finds fulfillment in her varied responsibilities and roles.

Right away, you sense God's affirming respect as the writer introduces this woman as "an excellent wife." She is rare, for he asks, "Who can find" one with such magnificent qualities? And in case you wonder if you are valued in God's eyes, just ponder this statement: ". . . for her worth is far above jewels" (31:10b).

Her relationship with her husband is nothing short of delightful:

> The heart of her husband trusts in her,
> And he will have no lack of gain.
> She does him good and not evil
> All the days of her life. [31:11–12]

> Her husband is known in the gates,
> When he sits among the elders of the land. [31:23]

> Her children rise up and bless her;
> Her husband also, and he praises her, saying:
> "Many daughters have done nobly,
> But you excel them all." [31:28–29]

There are affirmation and respect in those words. There is also supportive companionship, which causes this woman to work *with* her man, not against him . . . to do him "good and not evil" as she remains his partner.

I find this same woman quite capable. Perhaps a better word is *enterprising!* Look at the list of her activities mentioned from verses 13–27.

- She looks for good products.
- She works with her hands.
- She considers a field and buys it.
- She earns a wage.
- She plants a vineyard with her money.
- She makes her own clothes.
- She runs her own clothing business on the side.
- She is deeply committed to her home and family.

But this woman is not simply a "workhorse" . . . she is resourceful, compassionate, and secure. For example:

She is like merchant ships;
She brings her food from afar.
She rises also while it is still night,
And gives food to her household,
And portions to her maidens. [31:14–15]

She girds herself with strength,
And makes her arms strong.
She senses that her gain is good;
Her lamp does not go out at night. [vv. 17–18]

She extends her hand to the poor;
And she stretches out her hands to the needy.
She is not afraid of the snow for her household,
For all her household are clothed with scarlet. [vv. 20–21]

Give her the product of her hands,
And let her works praise her in the gates. [v. 31]

Within the heart of this mother is a depth of character.

Strength and dignity are her clothing,
And she smiles at the future.
She opens her mouth in wisdom,
And the teaching of kindness is on her tongue. [31:25–26]

"Many daughters have done nobly,
But you excel them all." [v. 29]

What a beautiful portrait! Can't you see her smiling as she looks toward the distant horizon of her life? She is neither insecure nor afraid. Her world is bigger than the immediate demands of today. Her strength is an inner strength, a sense of confidence in God. No wonder her children ultimately "bless her"! No wonder her husband happily "praises her"!

On top of it all she "fears the Lord." She walks with God. She holds Him in highest regard. She maintains a close relationship with the One who gave her her life, her health, her personality, her husband, her children, her ideas, her creativity, her determination to excel.

Somehow, you get the impression that this woman does not feel like a victim of four walls, a slave to a husband and houseful of kids. She certainly is no social invalid who feels inadequate and overwhelmed. No, not in the least. She has found some of the secrets of being herself, yet remaining extremely involved with and committed to her family, of enjoying her husband and the children, yet finding another dimension of fulfillment beyond them. And it's not because she is rich with servants at each door. Remember, she does her own shopping, makes her own clothes, works for a wage, and looks well to the many ways of her household. Quite a lady!

And may I add another dimension that is implied but not mentioned here? She is married to some kind of man! He must be incredibly secure and truly generous. He is not only willing to let her find fulfillment beyond him . . . he *affirms* her doing so. Don't forget, he praises her; he openly declares:

> "Many daughters have done nobly,
> But you excel them all." [31:29]

This man is worth a second look, fellow husbands. Maybe it is just male ego on my part, but I believe part of the reason why this "excellent wife," who was worth more than precious jewels, found fulfillment in her role as wife, mother, businesswoman, seamstress, investor, hostess, and friend of the needy was that her husband supported and affirmed such things in her. He found delight in her activities. He encouraged her to be the best mother possible, to reach out to others, to be all God meant her to be.

For those women who are blessed with partners like that, motherhood is a glory, not a grind.

 EFLECTIONS
ON MOTHERHOOD

1. Go back over these sayings in Proverbs 31. Take your time. Do a little honest appraisal. If you are a woman, take note of several behind-the-scene secrets of this woman's life.

   • Her positive attitude
   • Her indomitable spirit
   • Her secure determination
   • Her boundless energy
   • Her inner strength

   If you are a husband, review the comments I made in the next-to-last paragraph of this chapter. Are you like that? What could be done to help you be more of a support and encouragement?

2. In what ways are you gifted or skilled? Are you a good cook? Do you enjoy venturing into new (and sometimes risky) areas? Are you insightful as a counselor or teacher? How about sewing . . . are you a proficient seamstress? Does the idea of a small business intrigue you—say one you could do out of your home? Could it be that you have become so immersed in the daily demands of just "mothering," you have somehow lost the creative joys of being a whole person? Discuss this with your husband and/or a good friend.

3. Finally, think about the level of your commitment to the home. Do you really—honestly and truly—look well to the ways of your household? Do they know—does each member of your family realize—how much you value them and how committed you are to them? Could there be something you might do or change or say to communicate how deeply you care? Don't wait. Before the week has passed, fulfill that objective.

There are six things which the
    Lord hates,
    Yes, seven which are an
      abomination to Him:
Haughty eyes, a lying tongue,
And hands that shed innocent blood.
A heart that devises wicked plans,
Feet that run rapidly to evil,
A false witness who utters lies,
And one who spreads strife among
    brothers. [6:16–19]

THE GRIND OF DISPLEASING GOD

Even though we have mentioned various shades of this subject and have glanced at these sayings on more than one occasion in our study together, we need to face the music directly. Who hasn't struggled with the daily grind of displeasing the Lord? Is there a grind that brings greater ache of soul? I don't think so.

No one begins the day thinking about how he (or she) might displease God. On the contrary, most people I know face the dawn with high hopes of pleasing Him. In our minds we establish a game plan that will include a good attitude, a day of wholesome activities. We prepare ourselves for possible temptations and trials by meeting early with our God and giving Him our day in advance. And yet . . . before the morning is half done, we can fall into a syndrome of carnality that is downright discouraging, if not altogether demoralizing.

Perhaps it will help us this week to focus in on a specific target. Rather than praying in general terms, "Lord, help me to please You," it may be more beneficial to name seven specific areas where we need help. The list of seven is inspired— Solomon calls them the "seven which are an abomination" to our Lord. At the end of each of the seven discussions that follow, you will find a suggested prayer.

1. Haughty eyes. Our eyes reveal the truth of our souls. They convey so many of our unspoken emotions. Eyes announce anger, impatience, sorrow, sarcasm, guilt, and especially pride. It's that last one God hates with intensity.

"God, guard me all this week from hidden arrogance!"

2. A lying tongue. Not all lies are big and bold. Half-truths flow so freely. Exaggerations, too. And false words of flattery are commonly heard. Since we looked at the tongue so closely in Book I, have you been more conscious of your words? Are you more aware of your tongue's power?

"God, alert me to the destructive force of my tongue. Stop me from every form of lying!"

3. Hands that shed innocent blood. Solomon clearly states that the Lord considers murder an abomination. You may have been victimized by someone. It could be going on right now. As time passes, unless forgiveness replaces resentment, your bitterness could grow into rage . . . and you could "shed innocent blood." You may have a major battle with abusing your child. If so, you *must* get help!

"God, direct me to wholesome and healthy ways to solve and dissolve my uncontrolled anger. Keep me from the sin of shedding innocent blood!"

4. A heart that devises wicked plans. Because we have examined the heart so carefully, we are aware of its power and its importance. Nothing we do or say occurs until it has been filtered through the heart within us. It is there that "wicked plans" are laid. It is there we map out our yielding to temptation, our release of restraint, our scheme to get even with someone else.

"God, cleanse my heart from any hurtful way . . . remove every ugly thought or scheme I have been pondering!"

5. Feet that run rapidly to evil. Old habits are hard to break. Because we have "gotten away with it" before, the skids of sin are greased. In fact, we become increasingly less fearful of God's stepping in the longer we get away with continued, familiar paths of sin. "Because God does not punish sinners instantly, people feel it is safe to do wrong" (Eccles. 8:11, TLB).

"God, halt me in my tracks!"

6. A false witness who utters lies. Rare are the truth tellers. Many are those who deliberately misrepresent the facts. When we have the opportunity to defend another's character or set the record straight in a group that is bad-mouthing a certain individual, the temptation to chime in and agree (or remain silent and allow the character assassination to continue) is great. But the Lord *hates* such actions.

"God, free me from whatever fears I have so that my witness will be true, based on accurate facts!"

7. <u>One who spreads strife among brothers.</u> Juicy information is so difficult to contain. This is especially true if there is an element of verbal malignancy in the talk. How easy to "spread strife" among our brothers and sisters . . . how hard to be a peacemaker! But Solomon pulls no punches. He calls this one of those abominations God despises. This is the third in the list having to do with the tongue.

"God, silence me from any hint of gossip!"

We frequently think of the love of God, but all too seldom meditate on the things He hates. We should! Believe me, when God's Word says He hates these things, there is intensity in the statement. That means each one deserves an intensity of our effort to correct and control each one named.

EFLECTIONS ON DISPLEASING GOD

1. Go back to the closing prayers in each of the seven areas mentioned in the sayings. Interestingly, there are *seven* specific things God hates . . . one for each day in the week. You can probably anticipate this project. On Sunday, take that first subject area on God's "hate list" (*haughty eyes*) and pray the prayer I've suggested throughout the day. Concentrate on overcoming that all day Sunday. On Monday, take the second; Tuesday, the third . . . follow the plan all week long.

2. Since three of these seven have to do with the tongue, we must give great attention to this powerful force. All week pay special attention not only to what you say but how and when you say it . . . and why . . . and to whom. Talk less and say more.

3. Which one thing mentioned in the list could be called your most frequent battleground? Be absolutely relentless as you roll up your sleeves and take on this hateful, ugly enemy of righteousness. Displeasing God is habit-forming! But so can be our pleasing Him. Tell at least two other people of your major struggle. Request their prayers. Trust God to use their intercession and your concentrated effort to defeat this enemy.

PROVERBS

The proverbs of Solomon the son
    of David, king of Israel:
To know wisdom and instruction,
To discern the sayings of
    understanding,
To receive instruction in wise behavior,
Righteousness, justice and equity;
To give prudence to the naive,
To the youth knowledge and discretion,
A wise man will hear and increase in
    learning,
And a man of understanding will acquire
    wise counsel,
To understand a proverb and a figure,
The words of the wise and their riddles.

The fear of the Lord is the beginning of
    knowledge;
Fools despise wisdom and instruction.

Hear, my son, your father's instruction,
And do not forsake your mother's
    teaching;
Indeed, they are a graceful wreath to
    your head,
And ornaments about your neck.
My son, if sinners entice you,
Do not consent.
If they say, "Come with us,
Let us lie in wait for blood,
Let us ambush the innocent without
    cause;
Let us swallow them alive like Sheol,
Even whole, as those who go down to the
    pit;

We shall find all kinds of precious.
    wealth,
We shall fill our houses with spoil;
Throw in your lot with us,
We shall all have one purse."
My son do not walk in the way with
    them.
Keep your feet from their path,
For their feet run to evil,
And they hasten to shed blood.
Indeed, it is useless to spread the net
In the eyes of any bird;
But they lie in wait for their own blood;
They ambush their own lives.
So are the ways of everyone who gains
    by violence;
It takes away the life of its possessors.

Wisdom shouts in the street,
She lifts her voice in the square;
At the head of the noisy streets she cries
    out;
At the entrance of the gates in the city,
    she utters her sayings:
"How long, O naive ones, will you love
    simplicity?
And scoffers delight themselves in
    scoffing,
And fools hate knowledge?
Turn to my reproof,
Behold, I will pour out my spirit on you;
I will make my words known to
    you." [1:1–23]

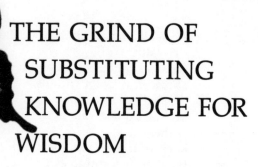

THE GRIND OF SUBSTITUTING KNOWLEDGE FOR WISDOM

Many, many weeks ago in Book I, when we first looked at the sayings of Scripture we began with the first chapter of Proverbs. It occurs to me that it would be worthwhile to return to it for a final time as we consider our tendency to *substitute knowledge for wisdom*. This is not only a daily grind; it is a lifetime tendency!

How easy it is to acquire knowledge, yet how difficult and painstaking is the process of gaining wisdom. Man gives knowledge; God gives wisdom. Knowledge is gleaned from getting an education—either by listening to and reading what the learned have to say or simply by gathering facts here and yon from your own experience. But what about the wisdom that is from above? As you already know, there is no course, no school, no earthly reservoir where such can be received. Unlike knowledge which can be measured in objective analyses and IQ tests and rewarded with diplomas and degrees, wisdom defies measurement; it is much more subjective, takes far more time, and has a great deal to do with attitude. One can be knowledgeable, yet distant from the living God. But those who are wise not only know the Lord by faith in His Son, Jesus Christ, they also hold Him in awesome respect. "The fear of the Lord" is still a telltale mark of wisdom.

So how does one obtain wisdom? Now that we have come to an end of our search through the sayings of Scripture, how can we continue our pursuit of God's wisdom? What are some ways to guard against falling back into our habit of substituting knowledge for wisdom?

I have four thoughts to suggest:

1. Read the Book of Proverbs regularly.

> The proverbs of Solomon the son of David, king of Israel:
> To know wisdom and instruction,
> To discern the sayings of understanding,
> To receive instruction in wise behavior,
> Righteousness, justice and equity;
> To give prudence to the naive,
> To the youth knowledge and discretion,
> A wise man will hear and increase in learning,
> And a man of understanding will acquire wise counsel,
> To understand a proverb and a figure,
> The words of the wise and their riddles.
> The fear of the Lord is the beginning of knowledge;
> Fools despise wisdom and instruction. [vv. 1–7]

The Book of Proverbs has thirty-one chapters—a natural fit into each month. It includes descriptions of over 180 different types of people. There is no mumbo-jumbo, no Rubic's-cube theology to unscramble, no weird, abstract theories to unravel, just straight talk for all of us who live imperfect lives on Planet Earth. Since Solomon declares that his writings have been recorded to help us "know wisdom," I suggest we take him up on it and glean new dimensions of wisdom by sitting at his feet. Read one chapter of the Book of Proverbs every day for the rest of your life and chances are good you'll not often be tempted to substitute knowledge for wisdom.

2. Hear and heed the counsel of those you respect.

> Hear, my son, your father's instruction,
> And do not forsake your mother's teaching;
> Indeed, they are a graceful wreath to your head,
> And ornaments about your neck. [vv. 8–9]

Wisdom isn't limited to the sayings of Scripture. It is possible that God has given you a godly set of parents, several trusted mentors, and one or two wise friends. They have been through

experiences and endured some trials you have not yet encountered. They have had time to weave all that through the varied
fabrics of life, which gives them a discernment and depth you
may lack. The things they can pass along to you are "a graceful
wreath . . . and ornaments" of wisdom available to you. Listen
to them. Learn from them. Linger with them.

3. Choose your friends carefully.

> My son, if sinners entice you,
> Do not consent.
> If they say, "Come with us,
> Let us lie in wait for blood,
> Let us ambush the innocent without cause;
> Let us swallow them alive like Sheol,
> Even whole, as those who go down to the pit;
> We shall find all kinds of precious wealth,
> We shall fill our houses with spoil;
> Throw in your lot with us,
> We shall all have one purse,"
> My son do not walk in the way with them.
> Keep your feet from their path,
> For their feet run to evil,
> And they hasten to shed blood.
> Indeed, it is useless to spread the net
> In the eyes of any bird;
> But they lie in wait for their own blood;
> They ambush their own lives.
> So are the ways of everyone who gains by violence;
> It takes away the life of its possessors. [vv. 10–19]

The longer I live the more careful I am with my choice of
friends. I have fewer than in my youthful years, but they are
deeper friends . . . treasured relationships.

As we read in Solomon's counsel, do not consent to relationships that drag you down and hurt your walk with God. Those
who "ambush their own lives" (v. 18) will get you involved in
counterproductive activities that will keep wisdom at arm's distance. You don't need that.

4. Pay close attention to life's reproofs.

Wisdom shouts in the street,
She lifts her voice in the square;
At the head of the noisy streets she cries out;
At the entrance of the gates in the city, she utters her sayings:
"How long, O naive ones, will you love simplicity?
And scoffers delight themselves in scoffing,
And fools hate knowledge?
Turn to my reproof,
Behold, I will pour out my spirit on you;
I will make my words known to you." [vv. 20–23]

If you have been on this journey since Book I, perhaps you recall the time we spent analyzing these words. Wisdom is personified as one who "shouts in the street" and "lifts her voice in the square." In other words, she is available. She speaks loud and clear. But, where? How? She tells us! "Turn to my reproof." It is there (in life's reproofs) she pours out her spirit on us and makes her words known to us.

God never wastes our time, allowing us to go through the dark and dismal valleys or endure those long and winding painful paths without purpose. In each one there are "reproofs" with wisdom attached. Many and foolish are those who simply grit their teeth and bear it. Few but wise are those who hear wisdom's voice and listen to her counsel.

For the rest of our years on this old earth, let's do our best to be numbered among that latter group.

EFLECTIONS ON SUBSTITUTING KNOWLEDGE FOR WISDOM

1. As we have discovered through the course of this book, the secret of memory is review, review, review. Today is a good day to set up a plan for reviewing the sayings of Solomon. If you wish to read through the Book of Proverbs on a daily basis, think about the best time and place for doing so. To keep the readings fresh, you might want to pick up a copy of the Scriptures in a different version or perhaps a paraphrase. As you read through the Book of Proverbs, you may also want to review some of the pertinent discussions in this book.

2. All of us have at least one wise person we really admire. If at all possible, arrange a time to get together . . . perhaps once a month or once every other month. If that won't work, how about listening to audio tapes that person has made or reading some things he (or she) has written? You may find that cultivating a close companionship and accountability with a small group of trusted friends is the best way to fulfill your desire for a life of wisdom.

3. As a final, end-of-the-book project, bow and thank the Lord for His faithfulness to you. His Word has been our guide. His mercy and grace, our encouragement. His love, our motivation. His Spirit, our Helper. His power to bring about changes within us, our hope. Express to Him how grateful you are for all He has taught you in these pages and for His patience with you as you attempt to live beyond the daily grind.

CONCLUSION

Perhaps it has been a full year since you began your journey with me through the songs and sayings in Scripture. At least that was my original plan for you as we set out together in our first week of reading with Book I. I hope you have learned as much as I have! In the process of gleaning truth, encouragement, insight, and renewed strength from the Psalms and the Proverbs, I hope you have come to know yourself better—a better understanding of one's self is always a byproduct of time spent in God's relevant revelation.

Most of all, however, I hope you have come to know our Lord in new and fresh ways—and have found Him to be interested in the nuts and bolts of your everyday existence. In fact, it seems there is nothing He is not interested in, certainly nothing He is not aware of! If He has the hair on our heads numbered, He must care intimately and intensely about the things that concern us . . . especially those daily grinds that eat away at us.

My objective all along has been twofold: first, to provide you with comments and explanations of the songs and sayings so you could have a better grasp of the biblical text; and second, to assist you with applications and suggestions of each so you could put the truth into action.

Nothing would please me more than to know that my objective was accomplished, namely, that you increased your knowledge of these immortal psalms and proverbs and that you have begun to turn that knowledge into wisdom in practical ways.

I must confess to you that when I began to write this book, I looked upon the assignment with a heavy sigh. The journey before me seemed long and arduous. I found myself struggling with (occasionally even *dreading!*) the exacting task of another book, especially a two-volume work of this magnitude. My "daily grind" became the writing of these volumes, strange as that may sound. But I knew they should be written. What a pleasant surprise awaited me!

The more I got into the work, the greater became my motivation. To tell you the truth, it wasn't long before I could hardly sleep due to my excitement. Ideas came with increasing, sometimes furious, speed. It got to the place where I could not write fast enough! The remarkable fact is that all this took place while I was getting as little as three and often not more than five hours of sleep a night. This took place while I was maintaining the leadership over the ministry of our church as well as doing some special projects with my daily radio outreach, "Insight for Living." And considering that I wrote this book immediately on the heels of my previous one, *Growing Wise in Family Life,* I have been all the more amazed at the energy and creativity that surged through me during the entire process. I realize now that I was being given a literal illustration of the message of this book. What I first saw as a demanding, pressing assignment God turned into a joyful, fulfilling, and growing experience.

Life is full of such serendipities. What we dread, He is able to transform . . . and frequently *does!* What we lack in energy or ability, He supplies in abundance. What we alone are unable to handle, He handles for us—His helping hand makes up the difference. The book you hold in your hands is a tangible proof of what you just read.

I am smiling as I write these concluding words; to my own surprise I have been the first recipient of blessing from this project. The songs and sayings I had hoped would help you have helped me already. The reflections that I felt might be of encouragement to you have been encouraging me for weeks. Of this I am certain: they work!

Now I can say beyond the shadow of a doubt that living beyond the daily grind is not just a title; it is reliable truth. It is, in fact, the life God has designed for us to live. That is why He gets all the glory for removing all the grind.

NOTES

Introduction

1. C. S. Lewis, *Reflections on the Psalms* (London: Geoffrey Bles, 1958), 2–3.

Section Three

1. In an unpublished speech by Dr. Howard G. Hendricks, Dallas Theological Seminary, Dallas, Texas.

2. A. W. Tozer, *The Pursuit of God*, special edition (Wheaton, IL: Tyndale House Publishers), 17–18.

3. Robert Robinson [1757], "Come Thou Fount of Every Blessing."

4. William O. Cushing [1823–1902], "Under His Wings."

5. Martin Luther [1529], "A Mighty Fortress," translated by Frederick H. Hedge [1805–1890].

6. Charles Haddon Spurgeon, *The Treasury of David*, vol. 2 (Byron Center, MI: Associated Publishers and Authors, 1970), 4:233.

7. Kenneth S. Wuest, *The New Testament, An Expanded Translation*, vol. 3 (Grand Rapids, MI: Wm. B. Eerdman's Publishing Company, 1959), 463.

8. Charles Haddon Spurgeon, *The Treasury of David*, vol. 2, 5:281, 282.

9. Daniel Webster, from the tract "The Book of All Others for Lawyers" by Henry G. Perry, published by American Tract Society, Oradell, New Jersey.

10. Charles R. Swindoll, *Growing Wise in Family Life* (Portland, OR: Multnomah Press, 1988).

11. Charles Haddon Spurgeon, *The Treasury of David*, vol. 2, 7:86.

12. Graham Scroggie, *The Psalms*, revised edition (London: Pickering & Inglis, 1948, 1965, 1967), 273.

13. F. B. Meyer, *Moses* (Grand Rapids, MI: Zondervan Publishing House, 1953, 1954), 31, 32.

14. F. B. Meyer, *Christ in Isaiah* (Grand Rapids, MI: Zondervan Publishing House, 1950), 9, 10.

15. A. W. Tozer, *Knowledge of the Holy* (Harper & Brothers Publishers, 1961), 61–63.

16. Annie Johnson Flint, "Pressed." From *Poems That Preach*, compiled by John R. Rice (Murfreesboro,TN: Sword of the Lord Publishers, 1952).

17. Charles Haddon Spurgeon, *The Treasury of David*, vol. 2, 7:229.

18. Charles Haddon Spurgeon, *The Treasury of David*, vol. 2, 7:293.

19. Charles Wesley [1707–1788], "O for a Heart to Praise My God."

Section Four

1. Augustine, *Confessions;* cited in *The Great Thoughts,* compiled by George Seldez (NY: Ballantine, 1985), 25.

2. Karl A. Menninger in *The Chosen* by Chaim Potok (frontispiece). A Fawcett Crest Book, published by Ballantine Books. Copyright 1967 by Chaim Potok.